THE LEADING EDGE

John Haggai, founder and president of Haggai Institute for
Advanced Leadership Training

THE
LEADING
EDGE

JOHN HAGGAI

WORD BOOKS
PUBLISHER
WACO, TEXAS

A DIVISION OF
WORD, INCORPORATED

Library of Congress Cataloging in Publication Data

Haggai, John Edmund
  The leading edge.

  1. Haggai Institute.   2. Missionaries—Training of.
I. Title.
BV2093.H26H34   1988   266'.007'152   ·   87–31639
ISBN 0–8499–0648–2
ISBN 0–8499–3114–2 (pbk.)

Printed in the United States of America
89801239FG987654321

To the men and women across the world who have served on the H. I. Boards, to the Executive Directors and other staff executives who have influenced Christian friends to undergird with their prayers, influence and money the globe-encircling ministry of Haggai Institute.

I thank God for their "work of faith, and labor of love, and patience of hope."

Christine Haggai

Contents

Foreword   9

Introduction   11

PART I: THE DREAM   19
Introduction / JCM   21
  1. God Gave the Dream   25
  2. God Refined the Dream   31
  3. God Actualized the Dream   37
  4. God Enlarges the Dream   43

PART II: THE PHILOSOPHY   49
Introduction / JCM   51
  5. Closed Doors Can Be a Blessing   57
  6. Work Hard; Pray Hard; Think Smart   65
  7. Traditional Ways Don't Work   75
  8. We Must Train Leaders   85
  9. Results Must Be Measured   95

PART III: THE PROGRAM   101
Introduction / JCM   103
  10. The Operation Must Have a Sharp Focus   107
  11. Finding an Acceptable Site   115

12. Recruiting the Best Staff   123
13. Private Funding Is the Only Way   137

PART IV: THE VISION   155
Introduction / JCM   157
14. The Past Is Prologue   159
15. Dreams Become Tormenting Visions   165

Foreword

For fifteen years Haggai Institute friends around the world insisted, "You must write the H. I. story while it's still fresh in your mind."

I didn't consider that a priority for two reasons: first, I simply didn't have the time, and second, I thought it might be misinterpreted as self-serving.

In 1979, I concluded something must be done. The leaders requesting the book were not frivolous people. At the mouths of so many witnesses "every word shall be established." So I discussed it with Dr. Michael Youssef, H. I.'s Executive Vice President and Managing Director. He said, "Let's have H. I. commission a professional author to write the book. That should circumvent your two objections."

Above all, I wanted a factual book that revealed the "warts and all."

After some six years of searching, in 1985 I met John C. McCollister whose qualifications were even better than we had agreed on. He had earned his Ph.D. in communications at Michigan State University. He had taught Greek, Theology, and *writing*. After his ordination to the Lutheran ministry, he had served several parishes. He had written ten books and hundreds of magazine articles. As if all that weren't enough, he currently serves as federal arbitrator for the FMCS (Federal Mediation and Conciliation Service) and the American Arbitration Association.

McCollister grasped the H. I. concept immediately. He came to both Singapore and to the Super Servant Seminar in Honolulu as guest lecturer.

After we had contacted him about writing and had come to a tentative agreement with Word Books, he read through the hundreds of pages I had written. After finishing the material, he phoned and said, "I'll write the overview chapters, organize the book, and edit your material, but it must come from you."

I read with awe as I ponder his insights and revel in his skill.

This book is only the tip of the iceberg, but it's honest—no puff. I salute Dr. John C. McCollister.

And, I must acknowledge with gratitude the editing skills of Miss Norma Byrd, my literary and research assistant, whom McCollister calls a "genius."

Throughout this text, certain names and places have been omitted to avoid political embarrassment for Christians in nations hostile to the gospel.

I pray God will use this to glorify Himself, convince non-Christians of our loving concern, challenge Christians and encourage them—especially the young—to pursue their God-given dreams, no matter what the obstacles.

JOHN HAGGAI

Introduction

"Attempt something so great for God that it's doomed to failure unless God be in it."

JOHN HAGGAI

Christine and John Haggai "on the way"

Introduction

This is the story of a man, his dream, and the world's most successful program for the worldwide proclamation of the gospel of Jesus the Christ.

The amazing chronicle of the Haggai Institute for Advanced Leadership is a playwright's Eden, overflowing with powerful dramas of contrasts. Its script portrays daring adventures and patient waiting; confident hopes and nerve-racking anxieties; unsolved mysteries and unqualified certainties; crushing failures and mountain-top victories. Its cast of characters lists bank presidents, supreme court justices, parish pastors, archbishops, military generals, psychologists, physicians, university professors, and other professionals who are bold enough to proclaim Christ as their personal Savior.

Since 1969, the story of the Haggai Institute has been presented on an international stage to standing-room-only audiences. Yet, until recently, most of us have never even heard of its existence.

The Haggai Institute wanted it that way.

The word "story" is purposely used in lieu of the common designation "history." A venture of this sort rarely has a history in the strict sense of the word. Instead, the record of the foundation and growth of the Haggai Institute more closely resembles a biography. Its every dimension mirrors the character of the man who created, nurtured, and guided it.

While many missionary organizations never get beyond the planning stage, those that are able to begin and survive do so amid fierce competition from unfriendly governments, other religions and, more often than not, even from those from within the fellowship of the Christian Church.

In spite of all the barriers thrown up to check their advance, all successful mission efforts share two legacies: a bold leader and priceless loyalty to the cause.

The Haggai Institute has both.

The Real Leader

John Haggai, the founder of "H. I.," is a leader who had an impossible dream, developed a pragmatic philosophy, initiated a marketable program, raised the necessary capital to fund a first-rate organization, and continues to envision yet more and higher mountains to climb.

Most leaders are never recognized until they die. Socrates, it is said, became a leader, or at least a hero, after committing suicide. Mozart was a respected court-sponsored musician, but remained unknown to the masses and was buried in an unmarked pauper's grave. Lincoln was honored by the majority of Americans only after his assassination. These men became famous after they were dead as a result of a particular philosophy which they enunciated.

Rare is the leader who is hailed by his contemporaries.

John Haggai is one of those exceptions.

Normally, a leader gains a following because he articulates a highly idealized approach to a problem. John Haggai takes the opposite view. He offers, instead, a simple, practical approach to world missions others try to emulate with little success.

Underlying the obvious simplicity of his approach lies a sophisticated organization of loyal men and women dedicated to the proposition that this is the only sensible answer to the challenge of the Great Commission:

Go, therefore, and make disciples of all nations, baptizing them in the name of the Father and of the Son and of the Holy Spirit, teaching them to observe all that I have commanded you (Matthew 28:18–19).

The command is clear. But, in the wisdom of God, we were never given specific instructions on how to do this.

What Most Churches Do

Most American Christian denominations train young men and women from all parts of the nation to equip them with the best methods of promoting the gospel to others living in Africa, Asia, Latin America, or the Middle East. But their rate of success is less than spectacular—not from lack of dedication or enthusiasm, but because their approach to evangelizing the faith carries with it the "Made in America" label.

Others have selected prime candidates from the nations to be served, brought them to the United States, educated them, and sent them home to their villages and cities to proclaim the Good News. That, too, hasn't worked as well as expected; all too often once the new missionary has returned to his native land, he meets even greater opposition. His education has made him so "Americanized," he is a complete stranger to his former family and friends.

A New Idea

John Haggai had a different idea. Instead of sharing the gospel via American-trained representatives, he asked himself, why not train the leaders of these nations on how to establish schools and Christian centers for the purpose of promoting the story of Christ and educating the people in living productive lives? "I was convinced the people to be trained must be top leaders," he says. "You build from the top down, not from the bottom up."

As leader of H. I., John Haggai has had to wear several
hats at once—as an administrator, a diplomat, a fund-raiser, a
speaker, a motivator, a counselor, and a writer. At the same
time, he never strived to be "all things to all people." He
maintained a solid stand for some fundamental principles—
even in the face of death.

The amazing truth about all this is that Haggai could have
been a success in the so-called "traditional" ministry as pastor
of a church. While he was a young minister at Ninth and O
Baptist Church in Louisville, Kentucky, his congregation led
every church in his denomination in the number of people who
professed Christ and followed the Lord in baptism. In 2½
years, 1,700 were received into the fellowship, including 1,000
by baptism. And that was from June 1954 until December
1956—a time when such gains were uncommon.

Seeing Beyond the Local Church

But unlike so many of his contemporaries, Haggai was
not interested in nurturing only his own flock. Thirteen mission churches were founded by his congregation. Also, the zeal
for world missions was always in the forefront of his mind. In
his first year at Ninth and O, for example, he raised the mission
budget from $16,000 to $106,000.

Over the next few years, his popular appeal as a preacher
through both the spoken and written word, reached far beyond
Louisville. He was invited to speak to congregations throughout America, then the world. It was on his first world journey
that Haggai became convinced the mission efforts of the
Church needed a fresh approach. His "top-down" theory could
only be realized through a solid organization in a location that
was politically acceptable to world leaders.

That place was Singapore.

A site was selected on Ridout Road, in the Embassy Sec-
tion; a building was bought and expanded; a faculty was selected, classes were taught; and world Christian leaders sent
forth. To this date, over 4,800 alumni have passed on their

training to more than 700,000 people in the Third World. Graduates include the head of the cathedral in Rio de Janeiro, a two-star general and the former head of Interpol in Indonesia, the Arab world's leading writer, several supreme court justices, a minister of foreign affairs, university presidents, pastors, bishops, archbishops, businessmen, and media leaders.

The obvious question is: Why haven't we heard about this before? John Haggai answers that himself. "The significance of any Christian ministry in a nation hostile to the gospel is inversely proportional to the exposure it gets in the West. Exposure in the West can mean expulsion in the East." That's why the work has been kept so quiet.

In spite of tremendous progress, the dream is far from over. John Haggai now envisions a "Singapore II" in Hawaii for training additional leaders in specialized studies on how to present Jesus Christ in a culturally relevant way.

Already scores of barriers have been thrown up to kill "Singapore II" even before the first shovel of dirt is turned. The frustrations are enough to discourage nearly anyone. But, after reading his story, you can't help but feel that in some way John Haggai, under God, will also turn this dream into yet another reality.

JOHN MCCOLLISTER

John Haggai—age 10—the year he dedicated his life to China

PART I

THE DREAM

Four generations—great-grandfather, grandfather, mother,
John Haggai at 4 1/2

Paul J. Meyer, world-acclaimed entrepreneur and founder of Success Motivation Institute, once commented to a struggling disciple: "If you are not making the progress you would like to make and are capable of making, it is simply because your goals are not clearly defined."

These are blunt words, but who can argue with them?

Assuming the truth of Paul Meyer's insight, we could turn the sentence around and draw the logical conclusion that if we *are* making the progress we would like to make, it is because our goals *are* clearly defined.

A Leader with a Goal

John Haggai's remarkable success in his unique ministry has been a direct result of clearly defined goals. And that goal wasn't a product of some flash-in-the-pan inspiration; instead, it was a commitment generating from a lifetime of prayer and study.

Young John was saved when he was only 4½ years old. This, too, wasn't the result of an instant divine revelation. "In fact, I can't even pinpoint the exact day or hour," he says. "I knew shortly before Thanksgiving, 1928, I had invited Jesus into my life, and my parents told me that the direction of my life changed."

The direction matured rather quickly. He felt the call to preach when he was only six. Four years later, he was convinced his ministry would be to serve his Lord and the Church as a missionary to China. "Why, I don't know," he says. "I certainly knew no Chinese people. However, the burden was heavy upon me, and I set my course."

That course wasn't without its share of pitfalls. The door to China was constantly being slammed shut. John's gifts and talents seemed to dictate that he head in another direction. On top of this, a near-fatal accident almost erased all possibility of any dream coming true.

But during those critical days, young John rededicated his life to serving the Lord. Although his high school aptitude tests indicated that he should enter the field of business, John enrolled in Moody Bible Institute. After graduation, he entered Furman University as he simultaneously pastored the Jackson Mill Baptist Church in Wellford, South Carolina. Full-time pastorates followed in South Carolina, Tennessee, and Kentucky.

By the standard criteria for successful pastors, John was at the top. His congregation in Kentucky, for example, led the nation in the number of people who professed Christ and followed the Lord in baptism. Yet, at the heart and core of his preaching and ministry was foreign missions.

That subconscious lure of missions, coupled with a not-so-gentle nudge from his wife, compelled John to cross the ocean to West Asia. What he saw was not what he had expected. America and its ideals were not inviting to the people of these lands. Instead, they were spirited with a new sense of nationalism. The writing was on the wall—if the Church were to make any impact on the Asians, it would have to recognize this truth and act accordingly. American missionaries could no longer be expected to gain large numbers of converts simply because both they and their message were branded with a "Made in America" label. It was not one that Asians were eager to wear.

Criticisms Abound

Throughout history, the Holy Christian Church has never been eager to change. This was no exception. When John returned home, he introduced his insights to Church leaders. He was turned aside with the backhanded remark: "Our way has worked in the past; it will work again." Some were even cruel in their remarks, accusing him of working against the Church.

Meanwhile, what most of his friends and enemies did not know was that Haggai's son—Johnny—was suffering from a terminal illness. No one could have blamed John were he to forsake his plans or put them on the back burner until this situation was resolved. But John Haggai is not one to let go of a good idea. In spite of personal sorrows and opposition from his colleagues and friends, he was convinced that a fresh, meaningful approach had to be utilized in a threefold manner:

First, people of the Third World would listen only to their own. Second, the most influential people—the leaders—would be the most effective. Finally, they could be trained only at a neutral site—some place free of controversial political ties.

On his own, John Haggai set in motion the plans for a training site in a neutral territory that would turn his dream into a reality. In 1969, with faith in God and the help of influential people, John discovered that a facility in Singapore could be made available. It has remained the center for training ever since.

What has happened since then is incredible. Over 4,800 national leaders have been trained here. The goal is to educate 10,000 by the year 2000. If every graduate trains 100 other Christian nationals (many of the current graduates have reached two and three times this number—one 12,000, another 16,000), the result is staggering—one million leaders will be trained for the preaching of the gospel!

Can any Christian denomination equal that mark in as short a time?

John Haggai is still dreaming. The essence of that dream is "Singapore II."

JCM

Haggai Institute's Cecil B. Day, Sr., Training Center in Singapore

1

God Gave the Dream

"Don't be a hypocrite. Don't say you are waiting for the Lord to lead you to go to the foreign mission field. How are you going to know His leading? Assume that He wants you to go to the foreign missionary field unless He closes the door."

PAUL FLEMING

The Reverend W. A. Haggai—"My father at age 90" (JH)

The experts said I was headed in the wrong direction. When the New York Regents began giving aptitude tests in the '30s, I was a freshman in high school. I scored at the top in the area of business ability. *Aha,* I thought to myself, *God wants me to be a businessman. I'll be the best businessman I can be, and I'll support a hundred missionaries.*

One of the reasons for my eagerness to enter business was that the image of the missionary was not glamorous. The average minister bored me out of my head. It seemed as though most of them were living with their heads in the clouds. Another reason for my less than enthusiastic endorsement of those who wore "the cloth" was the dire economic prognosis of the profession. Run-down parsonages, coupled with near poverty-level wages, promised little more than survival. I know. My father was a minister. And there were more than a few times when I saw this man's superior talents go unrewarded. I also recall seeing him distressed when he could not give us children some of the things enjoyed by our neighbors simply because there was no funding available.

Near Fatality

Suddenly, in 1940—when I was sixteen years old—
something occurred to change my attitude in a hurry. It was
the day after Christmas, 1940, when my friend and I were
riding in his roadster. Snow and ice covered parts of the road,
but my friend ignored the potential danger as he sharply
turned a corner at high speed. He lost control, and the car
rolled over. The flying windshield aimed for my thighs and
nearly severed my leg. For eight months I was off my feet.
Neither I nor the doctor were certain I would even keep my leg,
let alone be able to use it normally.

On top of this, the doctors and nurses continued to fill me
with sulfanilamide. Later, I was warned that the "cure" might
ultimately cause an aberration in the ratio of white corpuscles
to red corpuscles. That could lead to leukemia and an early
death—probably before I reached forty.

When you're facing death, you get your priorities in
proper relationship mighty fast. And you don't need thirty
days to pray over them.

But it was when I looked death squarely in the eye that I
determined to give my life to the will of the Lord. It wasn't that
making money was evil. It's good, even divine, if God has
called you to do that. But that wasn't what God wanted for me.
Instead, He wanted me to be directly involved in a ministry to
people.

After graduation from high school, I enrolled at Moody
Bible Institute. The course of study gave me the basics for the
gospel ministry. But in the back of my mind I knew that
the local church ministry in and of itself was not going to be
my life's ambition.

I could not identify with most clergymen—especially
with their preaching. Most of the sermons I heard were little
more than pleasant Sunday morning discourses. However, I
was fortunate to hear some giants of the pulpit—Dr. Robert G.
Lee, Bishop John Taylor Smith, Dr. J. C. Massee, Dr. W. B.

Riley, Dr. Porter Barrington, Dr. Harold Fickett, and Dr. R. S. Beal, for example—who would hold me spellbound, on the edge of my seat. For gripping Bible teaching, no one got my attention like my own father.

And there were missionaries such as Paul Metzler, Carl Tanis, and Paul Fleming who reinforced my commitment to preaching the gospel to the world. How was I to know for sure? What constituted that unmistakable call? With these questions resounding in my heart, Paul Fleming struck a particular chord as he seemingly spoke directly to me from the pulpit with the challenge: "Don't be a hypocrite. Don't say you are waiting for the Lord to lead you to go to the foreign mission field. How are you going to know His leading? Assume that He wants you to go to the foreign missionary field unless He closes the door."

Wow! That hit home.

But in 1949 the door to China slammed shut. Americans were thrown out. Missionaries were expelled. Marxists were now in control. My only alternative was to accept a call to a local church.

Mission Support

I was in the pastoral ministry for several years, serving churches in Lancaster, South Carolina, Chattanooga, Tennessee, and Louisville, Kentucky. God blessed those ministries. Even though I was not directly involved in missionary work, I did whatever I could to support the mission effort. Each of the churches led the way in mission giving.

The congregation of my first full-time church—Second Baptist Church in Lancaster—gave less than a thousand dollars to missions in 1948. In the next year, my first full year there, that figure jumped to $26,000. At Ninth and O Baptist Church in Louisville (my last pastorate), the mission budget in 1953 was $16,000. During my first year there in 1954, it swelled to over $106,000. The support of missions was on my heart.

But the local church ministry was a tremendous training ground for me. I learned the art and craft of prospecting, recruiting, and fund-raising.

It's true that Ninth and O Baptist Church led my denomination in the number of converts and baptism, but, if you can believe this, that still didn't excite me as it should. I knew why. I simply would never feel fulfilled until I became directly involved with missions. God had put a fire in my bones for world evangelism. I understood Wesley: "The world is my parish."

John and Christine Haggai—just married,
3 August, 1945, Chicago

2

God Refined
the Dream

"Today's answer to obeying the Great Commission is evangelizing THROUGH nationals TO nationals—nationals reaching their own people."

JOHN HAGGAI

John, Christine, and son Johnny

The degree of success in the local church ministry is in direct proportion to the extent of your prayer life, the number of hours you labor, and your ability to work with people. I not only prayed, I worked seven days a week from August 1945 until the end of 1964, and by the grace of God, I enjoyed an ever-growing fellowship with people I met along the way.

Meanwhile, my son Johnny was suffering the ravages of cerebral palsy, resulting from severe and unnecessary birth injuries. This, itself, was keeping my wife Chris confined to the house around the clock.

It was also tearing me apart. I wanted to be with them both through these long months, but my ministry to the congregation wouldn't permit me that luxury.

Christine knew that I had received an invitation to speak at St. Andrews University in Scotland. Normally, my wife is a reserved person. That's not to say she does not have her opinions. To the contrary. And more often than I want to admit, some of her ideas are better than mine. But she has never been one to express herself unless she is convinced that she's right. This time she spoke up loudly and clearly.

"If you continue this way, you're going to kill yourself. And where will that leave Johnny and me?" Then she offered a solution. "Take that trip to Scotland. And, when you're finished at St. Andrews, continue on through Europe to the Middle East and visit the land of your fathers."

Chris doesn't speak her mind that often, but when she does, she can be mighty convincing. The next day I arranged to take a three-week trip to Europe and West Asia.

Seeing the Third World

Europe was delightful. But it was what I saw in Asia that shocked me into a new awareness of reality.

Like many of my contemporaries, I thought that America was the nation to which the Third World looked with envy. That included everything from manufactured goods to educated missionaries. Instead, I discovered that people of the Third World had lost confidence in the lack of ethics they perceived in capitalism. And Communism, to them, had outlived its usefulness. There was a growing sense of nationalism that had never existed before in these nations.

When my father left Syria for the United States in 1912, for example, he had no loyalty to this former colony of Turkey. Today, Syria is a sovereign nation, and Syria has a nationalistic pride which equals that of any country.

It didn't take me long to realize two things. First, this neonationalism would mean that Westerners would be restricted, even prohibited, in many areas of the world. Second, the Church would have to adopt a different approach to its concept of missions.

In all this, God convinced me of one thing: *the answer to obeying the Great Commission is through nationals to nationals—nationals reaching their own people.*

An around-the-world trip I took in 1965 reinforced that belief. I saw the impact of Buddhism, Hinduism, and Islam. Adherents to these religions felt trapped. Their religion taught them they were not to make decisions, determine the course of their life, or even set goals. Although most of them never knew it, these people were striving for something that could only be found in Christ Jesus.

This became most apparent when I visited Indonesia. This nation successfully thwarted an attempted Communist takeover. But the victory was not without casualties. In the wake of that repulsion, the non-Chinese Indonesians erupted in hostility against the Chinese.

As in most Third World countries where you find Chinese, though they are in the minority, they control the wealth. Indonesia was no exception. The resentment turned into bloodshed. Within two years after the coup was aborted, 400,000 Indonesians were slaughtered. Most were ethnic Chinese. In one city of 50,000 population, over 30,000 people were beheaded and their cadavers thrown into the river, turning it crimson from the blood.

At the same time, an undercurrent of revival allowed the gospel to penetrate the walls of hatred and strife. The apostle Paul was right: "Where sin abounds, grace does much more abound."

The Indonesian experience reinforced my conviction that where Satan is the most aggressive, the Church has the greatest opportunities for spiritual victories. Satan, you see, does not concentrate on something already in his control.

Dr. Han Kyung Chik, to whom John Haggai dedicated his
book *Lead On!* —"The outstanding leader of my lifetime" (JH)

3

God Actualized
the Dream

"I refuse to bring these outstanding leaders . . . and put them in inadequate and shabby quarters just to prove to the world how 'humble' we are."

JOHN HAGGAI

Session 2, Switzerland

Based on my insights and the logical implications that followed, the truth became evident. No longer would these Third World countries roll out the red carpet for every American import—including missionaries. The prevailing new nationalism would not permit budding nations to admit to the rest of the world that they needed help from foreigners. They would much rather learn from their own people.

But what about the missionaries of the Church? They're still needed, but they must come in different colors.

No longer can we send missionaries who are American-bred and American-trained to such nations. This "Made in America" label must be removed from the promotion of the gospel. Otherwise, Jesus is pictured as someone wearing jeans, a ten-gallon hat, and cowboy boots. That's not relevant to someone from the Third World, whether he has lived his entire life in a thatched hut out in the bush, or in a marble palace in a bustling metropolis.

We Choose Leaders

If Christian leaders of those nations could be trained in promoting the gospel among their own, we could make much more progress.

Doesn't this make sense?

Why choose leaders instead of the common man and woman of the village? Because I am convinced you can build only from the top down, not from the bottom up.

Now, the question arose as to where we could train these leaders. Certainly we could not choose a location which would be politically offensive. It had to be at a neutral site.

Switzerland was our first choice. We planned to purchase a hotel, run it like a hotel during the peak season, then let the profits pay for our training program in the off-seasons.

It was a wonderful theory. We spent a large percentage of our income in 1968 for the procurement of an ideal hotel. At the last minute, the owner backed out of the agreement.

We located another facility—a beautiful chalet on Lake Brienz, near Interlocken. Again, more money was invested. But the owner pulled a financial double-cross. Had he done this in America, he would have been prosecuted. His own lawyer, in fact, admitted we had an open-and-shut case. My board members insisted we sue him. And we would have, had it not been for Dr. Han Kyung Chik.

This servant of God who started a church in Seoul, Korea, with only 28 refugees and built it to over 60,000 members, said to me: "Dr. Haggai, please do not sue. You may have every reason to. However, were you to sue a man whom Third World Christians consider to be your brother, it would be the end of your ministry in the Third World."

Heeding his advice, we walked away with a loss.

We moved our attention to another neutral site— Singapore. We arranged to conduct our first sessions on the nineteenth floor of the newly built Hyatt Singapore Hotel through my friend George Milne. Everything was set—or so I thought.

I arrived a few days prior to the first session. I was shocked. The hotel was not completed. Windows were not in; driveways were not completed; not one staff member was around, not even a sentry guard.

How was I to contact the thirty leaders and faculty who were now on their way? Where would they go once they saw the hotel? I was devastated. Again, God brought us through.

Expensive Costs

We needed to spend more money, but were able to lease a portion of the Singapore Forum Hotel. But even this decision flamed the ire of some critics.

The saintly David Adeney, former missionary to China and a respected leader of the Overseas Missionary Fellowship, said that putting Third World men in such plush facilities was sending a bad signal to other Christians. So, we spent one entire day looking for alternate facilities.

We found three. Two were more expensive than the space we were presently leasing; the other was 62 cents a day less. But none of these other places had air-conditioning. There were no elevators. We would have to put three or four men into one room. Food was inadequate. The Singapore Forum, on the other hand, provided telex facilities, typewriters, laundry service, two free lecture rooms, and a piano.

At the end of the day, I looked at my friend and said, "I refuse to bring these outstanding leaders who compare favorably with Billy Graham, Bill Bright, W. A. Criswell, Bishop Sheen, Robert LeTourneau, Cecil Day, Fred Smith, and Charlie Jones, and put them in inadequate and shabby quarters just to prove to the world how 'humble' we are."

This was not the only criticism I received. There was more—much more. Men whom I had admired for years were making statements such as, "This concept of John Haggai has put the cause of missions in reverse."

Clyde Taylor, a good and godly man whom I had known since I was twelve, said John Haggai had set the cause of missions back fifty years.

Others, who were as genuinely sincere, accused me of

throwing away God's money. They even criticized me for putting others on my staff.

Through all this, I recalled the insight of General Dwight Eisenhower: "There are no victories at bargain prices." To this I quote: "There is no pentecost without 'plenty-cost.'"

In spite of opposition, the dream was turned into reality. God had won another victory. But He was not through.

Congregation in Seoul, Korea, 1973—
John Haggai Evangelistic Crusade

4

God Enlarges
the Dream

"The significance of any Christian ministry in a nation hostile to the gospel is inversely proportional to the exposure it gets in the West."

JOHN HAGGAI

On steps of Young Nak Presbyterian Church,
Seoul, Korea, 1972—L-R: Dr. Han Kyung Chik,
Mr. James Frame, John Haggai

It's tempting to lie back and smell the roses. But there is much—so much—yet to be done.

Several months ago I was in London and gently accosted by some compassionate former missionaries to Asia and Africa: "How can you justify not having a training program here in London for those of us who want to reach the Third World influx that is inundating all of the United Kingdom?"

A few weeks later I met with my friend Jim Tutt and his mission pastor from the Evangelical Free Church in Fresno. "I have just been to Yugoslavia," said the Pastor. "The people from both eastern and western European countries have visa-free access to Yugoslavia."

Jim Tutt chimed in: "There is an opportunity here that's unparalleled in reaching Europe. We don't want to reinvent the wheel. We will underwrite anything you will do there."

"I'm interested," I said, "but, with all due respect, the least effective person to start a program in a situation such as this is an ordained clergyman. He should be a layman."

"We've got just the man," responded the pastor. "He's thirty-eight years old and a successful businessman. In addition, he reads, writes, and speaks twelve languages."

"Tell us what to do, and when you want to start a program in Yugoslavia," said Jim, "We'll underwrite it."

The China Challenge

Then there's China with its over 1.2 billion people. Our big underlying challenge is how to present Christ without compromise or offense.

Why is this H. I. approach so necessary? I'll say this only twice. The significance of any Christian ministry in a nation hostile to the gospel is inversely proportional to the exposure it gets in the West.

I repeat: The significance of any Christian ministry in a nation hostile to the gospel is inversely proportional to the exposure it gets in the West.

Simply stated, exposure in the West can mean expulsion in the East.

All three emphases—London, Yugoslavia, China—are true challenges, as are ministries to Africa and the subcontinent. But London and Yugoslavia must wait . . . at least for now. My priorities are focused on those nations where Christ is not known and the preparation of a Hawaiian center to accommodate Hawaii ("Singapore II"), and increasing the numbers from Third World nations.

Our center in Singapore has reached its maximum effective enrollment. We need, right now, an additional location in the free world which will provide a convenient location for leaders from South America and the Pacific Rim.

For political reasons, the mainland of the United States was out of the question. But Hawaii (America's Asian state), with its history and ideal climate, would be excellent.

Through the help of dedicated friends such as Hank and Dottie Bronson, Ben and Kathi Hoffiz, Tommy and Joyce Hill, Bob and Ruth Glaze, Polly and Dot Poole, Jack and Susanne Pinkerton, Paul and Jane Meyer, Bob and Charlotte Field, Susan Thacker, Elizabeth Kellerman, Alex and Belle Waterhouse, Rev. Abraham Akaka, Stan Mukai, Fred Gray, and the cooperation of many local government servants, we are underway in establishing a second center in Hawaii.

Years ago I heard someone say, "You can join the literary society and become informed. You can join the temperance society and be reformed. You can join society and become deformed. But only when you join Jesus Christ do you become transformed."

Future Dreams

How far and how fast will the ministry of H. I. grow? That depends on how *transformed* both staff and supporters become.

It's the kind of transformation exhibited by Russ Alit who studied with Dr. Han Kyung Chik—one of our senior faculty members. Alit returned to work among the people in Bali in Indonesia. He had to ford two rivers to reach two Stone-Age villages, where people lived a primitive existence. He taught them how to fish-farm, how to use solar heating, and how to turn pig manure into energy. Preceding any instruction on quality of living, Alit conducted Bible studies for the villagers.

Today, because of Alit's dedication, these people enjoy a better standard of living than most of their countrymen who live in big cities. He literally propelled them from the Stone Age to the twenty-first century.

But the amazing thing about all this was the fact that two of the villagers had beheaded Alit's brothers. The knowledge of their identity was a secret Alit kept from them for fear they might flee and never have the chance to hear the gospel.

At Haggai Institute, we don't need just dedicated people. We need zealots like Russ Alit.

Polly and Dot Poole with the late Dr. Ernest Watson,
dean emeritus of Haggai Institute

Part II

THE PHILOSOPHY

Dr. Paul Hiebert, honorary chairman of the international
faculty and lecturer on Cross-Cultural Communication

Jesus' parting challenge to His apostles prior to His ascension into Heaven was to make disciples of all nations. If Jesus said it, it can be done. And if it is not being done, it's not God's fault; it's our fault.

Nearly two millennia have passed since Jesus gave to the Church His "Great Commission." But the results, in the meantime, based on numbers, show a less than enthusiastic response to our Lord's Commission.

Several years ago, then heavyweight boxing champion Muhammad Ali boldly proclaimed: "I am more famous than Jesus Christ." His brashness appalled many Christians. They should have been appalled, but not for the obvious reason. Were they to examine the facts, they would have had to admit that Ali was correct. Due to an enormous amount of public relations, coupled with an abundance of hoopla, Ali's career has been followed by people everywhere. Pictures of him hang in their homes. His name and image are known by prince and pauper alike.

At the same time, in spite of the great advancements in the art of communication, nearly one-half of the earth's inhabitants have never heard of Jesus Christ. The nearly 970 million people of this world who claim to be Christians are but 20 percent of the earth's population.

One of the reasons for this shocking truth is that an estimated three-quarters of the Third World's people live in countries that either discourage or openly prohibit foreign missionary efforts. Yet we still read the Great Commission of Jesus to evangelize the world. What are we to do?

In his vigor for the proclamation of the Gospel, John Haggai was as frustrated as anyone about the lack of success by missionaries who were bound to follow the traditional manuals on how to preach the good news to Third World people. But, unlike most of his contemporaries, Haggai was not satisfied with wringing his hands and groaning in frustration. He developed a better way.

The Better Way

He took a hard look at the standard operations. Normally, the scenario ran something like this: A white, Western-trained missionary is sent into a nation of people who have lived their entire lives in a culture different from what he has seen. To work among these people, the missionary had two choices: to adapt to their environment, or to convert them to his way of living.

If the missionary chose the first approach, he usually made himself look as if he were trying to be something he wasn't; if he chose the second, he would soon discover the people were not prepared to give up their way of life—primitive as it might have been—just to satisfy some alien with a strange message.

Some denominations used a slightly different approach. Instead of sending in foreign missionaries, they selected some of the more intelligent young men from the nation and invited them to study in one of the fine schools of the United States or Europe. Upon completion of their college and seminary requirements, they were sent back to their native lands to preach the gospel.

This plan looked good on paper, but still did not work effectively. The new evangelists were now looked upon as another kind of foreign missionary. While they still possessed the physical appearance of their fellow nationals, they were considered "Twentieth Century Uncle Toms."

Something else had to be done.

In the thinking of John Haggai, the best means of reaching the people was through their own. The one who carried the message couldn't be just anyone. He or she had to be someone who had earned the respect of others.

It logically followed that the only way to penetrate these borders was through qualified Christian national leaders who are willing to carry on the work of the gospel within these closed nations.

Haggai put his philosophy into practice. The results were amazing—even to him.

Recognized Success

Dr. Paul Hiebert, veteran missionary and missions scholar, praised Haggai's approach to evangelism. Recently, he summarized his opinions before an assembly of Christian businessmen: "The lack of experienced national leaders has seriously hindered the growth of the Church throughout the Third World. The Haggai Institute is helping to fill this great need for properly trained Christian leaders. It is the only post-colonial model we have today for world evangelism."

In any team sport such as football, if you are losing games, you change your game plan. And the truth of the matter is we in the Christian Church have been losing the contest for souls, yet we continue calling the same signals.

The Haggai Institute has dared to change the game plan. Instead of sending Western-trained missionaries onto foreign soils, it invites evangelical leadership from throughout the world and, through interaction with the faculty, determine answers to the burning question: "How do I present Jesus Christ to my people without compromise and without offense?"

Let it be said, in all fairness, the Western Church must be commended for the introduction of new and effective tools for evangelization over the past half century.

Radio has been exploited for the glory of God.

Television, including satellite communications, reaches into many areas around the globe.

Audiovisual communications undergird the outreach of the gospel in many areas.

However, the greatest need is for cultural relevance. The imperative today is to recruit spiritually sensitive leaders who can relate to a particular audience in a culturally meaningful way, whether that audience be one or thousands. This requires meticulous research on the part of the staff, professional training by skilled faculty, and dedicated loyalty by those who respond to the words of Jesus' Great Commission.

What's in a Name?

At the same time, there are those who raise an eyebrow at the fact that the Institute carries the name of its leader and founder. Some have gone so far as to suggest this is an ego trip. Not so.

The Institute, formerly known as "Evangelism International," changed its name to Haggai Institute in 1974 because three other organizations had taken the "EI" name.

Although the Institute predated the other groups, the Board decided on a name change to circumvent the confusion of multiple Evangelism International organizations.

One of the trustees asked John Haggai, "Isn't your family name 'Haj' in Arabic? And doesn't it mean 'pilgrim'?"

Haggai responded, "Yes. Haj was the name given Muslims who had taken the pilgrimage to Mecca and to Christians when they had taken pilgrimages to the Holy Sepulcher. My great great grandfather made many pilgrimages to the Holy Sepulcher in the nineteenth century."

The trustees said, "Why don't we change the name of Evangelism International to Haggai Institute? Nobody will pirate that name."

Thus, the name Haggai Institute.

As evidenced hundreds of times, God sovereignly led in this choice. (And not only did it honor the man who initiated the plan, but the name "Institute" has proved to be an important factor.)

When Idi Amin was torturing and murdering thousands of Ugandans, an anesthesiologist, Dr. Kityo, came to Singapore for the Advanced Leadership Program. With misty eyes and a tremor in his voice, he told Haggai, "Thank God, your stationery makes no mention of a church, the Bible, evangelism, or Christianity. If it had, I could have been sent to prison, torture, even death. The government is sensitive about intellectuals leaving the country, but since Singapore is looked on as the brain export capital of the Third World, and I was leaving for 'Advanced Leadership,' they gave me my travel documents."

The philosophy of H. I. began and continues to hold as its number-one priority the promotion of the gospel of Jesus Christ in a way that is most effective in today's society. And it matters little to John Haggai, the Board, or any of its supporters how many "sacred cows" have to be slaughtered to get the job done.

JCM

Predecessor to Haggai Institute—Total Evangelism
Indonesia—departure of Jakarta, Indonesia

5

Closed Doors Can

Be a Blessing

"Lord, we thank you for bringing Dr. Haggai all across the waters to be with us. We realize he may be shot tonight, but we rest in Thy will."

PRAYER DURING INDONESIAN VISIT

Col. and Mrs. Ds. Soesilo, General John Huwae, and
John Haggai at Jakarta meeting. Col. Soesilo is former
chief of chaplains of the Indonesian Navy; General Huwae,
former head of Interpol for Indonesia. Both are 2nd session
H. I. alumni.

I nearly gave up a thousand times. Every time the Lord opened one door, it appeared two were slamming shut. But I remained convinced that a new, more effective approach to missions lay in the willingness of national leaders to gather for instruction on effective leadership and communication skills at a neutral site.

I was determined to put this philosophy into action.

Switzerland

In 1966, a colleague introduced me to his father who owned a hotel in the French-speaking sector of Switzerland and dreamed of using the facility for training evangelists. This, to me, was an ideal location for our program. I was convinced this was a blessing from God.

We were all set to finalize the purchase of the property, when, suddenly, twelve hours before we were to set pen to paper, our hopes were dashed. An architect from London had come up with suggestions for improvement of the property.

The owners agreed this was the way to go. Inexplicably, they reversed their decision. We were no longer in the picture.

Hundreds of hours invested and thousands of dollars spent seemed to go for naught. But God wastes nothing.

Partly out of frustration and partly because of a desperate need for help from above, I began a more intense study of the Bible—particularly of how God worked with His servants. I studied the lives of Moses, Jeremiah, and Nehemiah. Gradually, the truth revealed itself.

Although I had already known it theoretically, I now could internalize the truth that any work for God will be fought tenaciously by Satan and his hosts. I concluded that one of the weaknesses of Christians surfaces when the moment of opposition comes along. They throw up their arms and lament, "Oh, the Lord must not be in this. There is too much against us."

I don't know what Bible they're reading. I've seen no translation to refute the idea that when God is really at work, all hell breaks loose as Satan trains the forces of the infernal regions upon the project.

Indonesia

I was in my Atlanta office making final preparations for a major evangelistic thrust. This time I was headed for Indonesia, the world's fifth largest nation, where an unprecedented awakening reportedly was underway. Local clergy had invited me to come with a group of evangelists—clergy and laity. I had completed initial plans for this effort which was to climax in a crusade in Jakarta's Senajan Stadium.

On the day before my departure, fifty-six men and women who had been invited to take part in the project had flown to Seattle where I was to join them and then proceed with them to Indonesia. Late on the eve of my departure, I received a cablegram from Jakarta. The words leaped off the page:

> Do not bring group to Indonesia. You will be denied entry.
> Should you get through Customs, you will be denied hotel rooms
> at the Hotel Indonesia. Repeat: do not come.

What was I going to do? My heart sank at the fate that lay before us. The group had invested over $145,000. Those leaders—doctors, businessmen, clergymen—had wrenched their schedules to work in this trip. They were waiting for me at a hotel in Seattle. Failure to go to Indonesia would destroy my credibility and torpedo my ministry. I prayed fervently that God would show me what to do.

About two o'clock in the morning, I went to the refrigerator to pour a glass of milk. And that's strange, because I don't drink milk. But while I was opening the door, I thought to myself: "Aren't you the guy who wrote the book *How to Win over Worry?* Look at you. You're in shambles." I left the matter in the hands of God and got a good night's sleep.

The sharp ring of the telephone awakened me in the morning. It was a call from Western Union. "Ignore previous cable," read the operator. "God is on the throne. Anticipating arrival of you and the group."

I showered, dressed, closed my suitcase, rushed to the airport, and caught the plane to Seattle. That evening, a colleague and I directed the briefing with the group.

"I hear we are not going to be permitted in Indonesia," said one participant. "What shall we do? Isn't this a terrible risk we're taking and a terrible gamble with funds?"

I was astounded that this man had gotten hold of the information. Just as I was thinking of how to phrase my reply, Dr. Clarence Sands, Pastor of the great San Jose First Baptist Church, said, "Yeah, I heard the same thing from the same blabbermouth. We can't gauge our actions or determine our plans on irresponsible mouthings like this."

This was all that was necessary. We went to Indonesia and went through Immigration and Customs without a hitch. Our group got the finest accommodations in the Hotel Indonesia—the only air-conditioned hotel in equatorial West Java at that time.

Soon after we arrived, one of the Indonesian leaders asked, "How can you live with your conscience when you know that communicating the gospel of Jesus Christ could so antagonize the Muslims? Are you aware the Muslims burned twenty-nine churches in the Sulawesi Islands just a few weeks ago?"

How do you answer something like this? My response was quite simple:

1. If we predicate our response to God's directive to evangelize the world on fear, we'll never get anything done.

2. Indonesia is entering a new economic phase. The government is inviting people from all over the world—Christians, Hindus, Buddhists. If Indonesia is going to participate in the international market, they, of necessity, will be obliged to provide protection to people of non-Indonesian faiths.

3. One of the five pillars of the Indonesian Pancasila is "freedom of religion."

Suddenly, we heard another door slam shut. The stadium was not available. And we had only thirty hours before the first service of the crusade.

Rain from Heaven

Some local students were demonstrating in front of the stadium where our meetings were to take place. The students were allegedly demonstrating over the increase in the price of rice. But all Indonesians knew they were really protesting the Christian meeting at the stadium. It was the subtlest of subtle Oriental subterfuge.

This was supposed to be the area's dry season. But, for some unexplained reason, it rained torrents each day until 5 p.m. The rain made the demonstrating students head for cover. Our service was scheduled for 6:30. We proceeded on schedule.

Just before the first service, I met with the local committee. One man stood up and prayed: "Lord, we thank You for bringing Dr. Haggai all the way across the waters to be with us. We know he is in Your hands. We realize he may be shot tonight, but we rest in Thy will."

It was at this juncture I learned the real meaning of "Watch and pray." I opened one eye to watch, while I prayed with the other eye closed.

Following the prayer meeting, one of the committeemen, in a gesture to console me, said, "Don't worry, Brother Haggai. There are 250 plainclothesmen in the stadium."

I did some quick calculations. That meant one plainclothesman to every thirty-two people. That wasn't much comfort. I was a sitting duck for any terrorist. Nevertheless, I trusted the Lord and disregarded the fear factor. So, relying on God to calm me, I stepped up to the platform.

The crusade went off smoothly. Hundreds accepted Christ as their personal Savior. God interceded that night and during the remaining meetings. No one was harmed. Thousands entered into peace with God.

After I had returned to my hotel room, I was visited by Mr. Jusuf Setyiwan who insisted that I meet May and Bill Goei—his sister and brother-in-law—of Singapore. I made it a point to do so. For twenty years, they have supported the H. I. ministry through prayers, finances, and third-person contacts. Bill served for many years on the H. I. (Singapore) Board.

All this would not have been possible had the rain continued.

Was God a part of this? Draw your own conclusion.

Early stages of planning—Dr. Bob Pierce and John Haggai

6

Work Hard; Pray Hard; Think Smart

"I was determined never to strike a blow that I could not follow up with another blow."

JOHN WESLEY

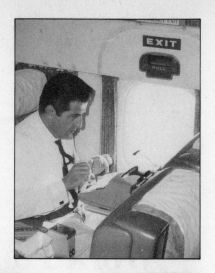

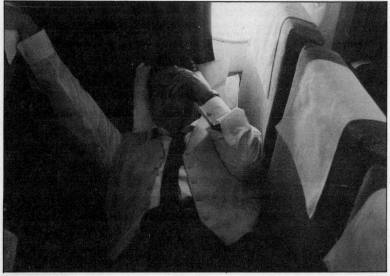

In travels oft

I had been virtually living on airplanes during those early years. To save money, I would fly at night and on arrival in the morning would negotiate with the hotel to let me have a room for two hours to take a bath, get my clothes ready for that day, then flop across the bed where I would sleep soundly for an hour, until the telephone operator gave me a wake-up call.

On occasion, I have traveled around the world in fifteen days, with few full nights in a bed. I would arrange my flights so I would arrive in one city after the last flight left for the next city. In this way, the airline was required to put me up for the night, handle the transportation fare to and from the hotel, and pay for my meals until the next flight out.

I would arrange to arrive in Tokyo at night, minutes after the last flight left for Hong Kong. Thus, Pan Am would put me up at the Keio Plaza Hotel. I arranged meetings from 9 p.m. until 2 in the morning with the Japanese whom I needed to see. Five hours later, I conducted another meeting until I had to leave for the airport at 10 a.m.

When I could not make arrangements such as this, I would sleep on the airplane, then work during the day, saving both time and expense.

Other Burdens

As I was hopping around the world, Johnny was back home hovering between life and death. Conditions at home were delicate, to put it mildly. My wife felt I should cut down on my travel not only for the sake of my health, but also so I could spend more time with Johnny.

Handling the demands of Johnny, which his cerebral palsy and accompanying paralysis imposed, Christine was carrying a terrific burden. Even when I was home, she knew my mind was on a multitude of demands. She knew, even when I was talking with the family, my mind was on the next action I needed to take to keep the ministry from dying a-borning.

I told her that within twelve months I thought the work would be in good enough shape so I could cut down some of this frenetic, kinetic activity. In one of those heart-to-heart conversations I told her, "Honey, God has made sensitive to this work some people whose gifts will help alleviate the pressure. And I really believe I'll be able to reduce my work load by twenty percent by the end of the year."

But, I didn't expect one decision from Washington, D.C., would have such an impact on our ministry.

In August of '71, President Nixon cut the dollar loose from gold and let it float. It had the same effect as a devaluation of the dollar.

On the morning of August 15, one American dollar would buy 3.33 Singapore dollars. Within four short months, one American dollar would buy only 2.4 Singapore dollars. That had an effect of nearly doubling our financial needs. Even though I had told my wife in all good faith I would be able to slow down, for the next eighteen months I worked harder than I had ever worked in my life.

How God sustained me physically was a matter of gratitude I expressed to Him in private prayer but never mentioned to anyone else. Here I was, forty-seven years old, and I saw no light at the end of the tunnel in terms of relief.

I spoke to many people about assisting with the H. I.

ministry. They were polite, but few of them were interested in risking a solid position in a traditional church or institution for a much greater challenge that could not be proved.

But there were those who did offer support for this unproved "experiment" in missions. I will forever give gratitude to those people—especially the Board members—who helped me through those difficult days when there was little track record.

While I thank God for the victories of those early days, I was learning what to do and what not to do. I had no rule book. There was no software program into which any of us could plug our numbers. There were people such as J. L. Nevius, Roland Allen, John R. Mott, and others who, over the years, asserted the need for indigenous evangelism in the non-Christian world. But no one had the answer to the "how."

We knew this, however: We had to pray as if everything depended on God, and work as if everything depended on us.

After one of our seminars on evangelism in Tretes—in East Java, Indonesia—we identified several Indonesian leaders whom we would bring to the first international seminar, wherever and whenever that would be.

Developing a Philosophy

My philosophy of missions, in the meantime, was being refined. I drew some bedrock conclusions:

1. "He who does the work is not so profitably employed as he who multiplies the doers." (A quote in 1818 by a man named Morley.)
2. Taking Westerners to Third World churches to format the program and lead the evangelistic endeavors, while no doubt beneficial, was not as effective as using Third World leaders to do the same work, even if they were from other countries.
3. The music, the format, and all activities associated

with the evangelism thrust must be consistent with local culture.

John Calvin correctly asserted that of all the fields of knowledge, the two most important are the knowledge of God and the knowledge of man. The pattern in the West, however, has been to export the gospel within a Western cultural framework, while ignoring the knowledge of man. Too often, well-meaning Westerners have done damage through their total insensitivity to cultural mores of the non-West.

In many areas, resentment is not directed to the person of Jesus the Christ, but rather to Western domination. Many non-Western people consider the approach of traditional missionaries to be nothing short of cultural colonialism and ideological imperialism.

In his book *Integrity,* Ted W. Engstrom (with Robert C. Larson) relates a story by his friend and associate in World Vision Tom Houston:

"In the late sixties, Alan Redpath visited us in Nairobi. He had been seeing Africa only through white missionary eyes. One evening I invited a group of black leaders to our home to have a meal with him and Marjorie. As he listened to their perspective on the missionary story, he became increasingly frustrated until he burst out and said, 'Did we do nothing right?'

"Then there was a pause, and one man, Daniel Wacko by name, said, 'Yes, yes. You did do something right. You gave us the standard by which to judge you. If you had not shown us the truth of Christ, you would not have put yourself so badly in the dark.'"

Have the Western missionaries and the churches that send them really done their homework as they should?

Let's face it. No business worth its salt would attempt to merchandise goods or services today without adequate market research. Christian organizations have been derelict in researching the market. They have failed to identify and understand the peoples they're trying to reach.

Some Western pastors will still shout from their pulpits:

"We have years of experience." But experience is not necessarily the answer. "Practice makes perfect," is a familiar guideline; but lousy practice makes something perfectly lousy.

The West has too often functioned much like the fledgling student of a foreign language. He considers what he wants to say in English, then tries to translate it into the foreign language. Compare this to someone proficient in a foreign language who begins to think in that language.

Too often, the West has laid out its objective, formulated its plan, then, to its own undoing, attempted to impose this Western format on Easterners.

The Easterner's resentment often eludes the Westerner. For one thing, the people of Asia are unspeakably polite. They would never do anything to cause another to "lose face." So the Westerner returns, thoroughly convinced his message has been "bought" simply because it was met with a smile and apparent acquiescence. He does not realize that behind this smile may be disdain by the listener who says to himself: "Such effrontery! How dare he come with an arrogant know-it-all attitude from a country only two hundred years old and try to teach basic truths to people with a five-thousand-year-old culture?"

In 1955, Indian Prime Minister Jawaharlal Nehru asked Bob Pierce, founder and at that time president of World Vision, "Do you believe that Christianity is self-propagating?" Bob responded with an emphatic, "Of course."

"Are you aware, Dr. Pierce, that the apostle Thomas brought Christianity to India's Malabar Coast in 52 A.D.?"

"Yes, and I am aware that he died in India, where tradition tells us he was slain by a dart in the vicinity of Madras."

"That's correct. Now, my question is, if Christianity is self-propagating, and if Christianity came to India more than 1,900 years ago, why is it you found it necessary to prop up your religion with 9,000 foreign missionaries today?"

When Bob was recounting this experience, I listened with the same awe that must have captured him at the time of the Nehru meeting. "Bob," I asked, "what did you answer?"

"Fortunately, there was an interruption, but, John, he made his point."

Think about Paul the apostle. He was never guilty of this travesty. He never imposed the structures, the organizational format, or the cultural mores of one culture on another. He never imported permanent personnel or finances to maintain an ongoing ministry when he moved to a city in his missionary effort. He was in Thessalonica only two weeks, "Three Sabbaths." He left no capital fund, no foreign personnel. The only possible exception to the conclusion that Paul did not import foreign personnel is that Timothy apparently stayed in Ephesus and Macedonia for extended periods of time.

It is true that Paul had asked the Church at Corinth to take up a collection to help the poverty-stricken Church in Jerusalem. A year later, when he returned to collect the money, they had not raised it.

Paul never indigenized the essence of Christ's gospel, but he always indigenized the expression of that essence.

He commended the Romans that ". . . your faith is spoken of throughout the whole world" (Romans 1:8b KJV).

And he could say to the Thessalonians, "For from you sounded out the word of the Lord not only in Macedonia and Achaia, but also in every place your faith to God-ward is spread abroad; so that we need not to speak any thing" (1 Thessalonians 1:8 KJV).

Nehru's question of Bob Pierce still begs for an answer.

John Wesley once said, "I was determined never to strike a blow that I could not follow up with another blow." Slowly I was beginning to learn it was better to go fewer places and keep following up the blows struck for God with other blows that would deepen the impact. But I was convinced the only way to do this was to fight in the arena of the nationals and to obey their rules.

A Humbling Lesson

One of America's respected Christian leaders went with me to Indonesia several years ago to visit a large and dynamic church. My American friend presumed to suggest to the pastor of that church ways in which he could improve his effectiveness for the Lord. He suggested Sunday school be conducted at 9:30 a.m., followed by morning worship at 11. Perhaps there could be a training period at 6 that night, followed by a 7:30 evening evangelistic service.

I said nothing, but I was dying inside.

The Indonesian pastor listened patiently to every word. A typical Indonesian might have responded: "It was so gracious of you to come here and share these wonderful ideas with me." But my Indonesian friend had taken five years of postgraduate work in the United States and was keenly aware of the American mentality. He looked my American friend in the eye as he smilingly asked the simple question: "Why?"

That rocked the American back on his heels. Before he could think of an answer, the Indonesian pastor graciously said, "We have a service at six o'clock Sunday morning for saints; we have one at nine o'clock for sinners. You Americans try to feed sheep and convert goats at the same time. We have separate services. In between, we have Sunday school at seven-thirty, which draws both groups. Do you have something better than that?"

The American was tongue-tied.

The Indonesian pastor continued. "What time do your people in America get up on Sunday morning?" he asked.

"Uh . . . about eight-thirty or nine o'clock," said the American.

"Our people get up between four and four-thirty in the morning," said the Indonesian. "It gets very hot here, and we don't have air-conditioning." He went on with the rationale for his church format. All the while he was sweet, gentle, and considerate.

As we left, the American said to me, "I don't think it was a wise thing I did in suggesting he adopt our Western procedure and structure."

I assured him he had learned a valuable lesson which the majority of Westerners never seem to learn.

John Haggai and the late Egyptian President Anwar Sadat

7

Traditional Ways
Don't Work

*"Many people from the West are willing to sacrifice their lives
for the sake of the gospel, but they are not willing to sacrifice
their thoughts."*

FRED THOMAS

John Haggai with the late Indian Prime Minister Indira Gandhi

During that 1964 visit to West Asia, nationals confronted me with an earnest plea. "John," they said, "we love the missionaries of the Church, but they treat us like children. We are not satisfied to be marionettes on the end of a Western string. That offends us. The work of God suffers because we are not treated as equals. The missionaries love us; they're willing to die for us, but they are not willing to share the ministry."

Frankly, I was angered at their statements. I eulogized the missionaries. I told these nationals how God had used the missionaries to bring hope and help to people of many generations—including my father and his Damascus family. I reflected on the great sacrifice missionaries had made. I reminded them that from the late eighteenth century until 1960, one out of every four members of missionary families in India had died during foreign service. How could they question the methods of people willing to die for their commitment? "And they love you so much," I argued.

Apologetically, they responded, "We love them, too, but their paternalism stifles the growth of the Church. Many of our people are offended and refuse to come to Church because of the way the Westerners take charge. They're not rejecting Jesus; they're rejecting Western domination."

Several of the more aware missionaries sensed this resentment and asked me to act as a mediator of sorts. "John, talk to some of these nationals," begged one. "Tell them we can't turn everything over to them willy-nilly. We have to answer to our denomination boards back home."

There was the dilemma. West Asia had developed its own neo-nationalism. During the preceding 19 years, more than 100 new nations had gained independence and sovereignty. Patriotic zeal is highest whenever a colony becomes a sovereign nation. At the same time, the missionaries were sent by their denomination boards with specific—often outdated—instructions on how to conduct their mission efforts.

It was clear to me the nationals viewed foreign mission work as foreign interference. Therefore, the obvious conclusion was to encourage Christian national leaders to teach their fellow countrymen about the Christian faith.

Surely, I thought, *someone has considered this before.*

We Expect Few Results

Have you ever had an idea that was so obvious, so simple, you concluded: "If there were any value in this idea, surely other people would have acted on it before now"? That's what was going through my mind. "I must be missing something. If what I perceive to be true is, in fact, the truth, surely others have already addressed themselves to the problem and are working fervently toward its solution."

But they haven't. The truth is they are using old methods in an attempt to solve modern problems.

In addition, a lingering pride somehow compels the Westerner to conclude his philosophy and approach to life are the only ideals worth promoting.

In 1979, an alumnus of Haggai Institute, Mr. Fred

Thomas of Indonesia, gave a perceptive answer: "Many people from the West are willing to sacrifice their lives for the sake of the gospel," he said, "but they are not willing to sacrifice their thoughts."

Ouch! That struck a nerve.

Consider an American couple who have surrendered to do missionary service in a strange land. They go to a desert area. They are not conditioned to the climate nor to the food. They struggle with the elements of nature, even as they struggle in their effort to master the language and to understand the culture. They labor for twenty-seven years, interspersed every four years with a one-year furlough. After twenty-seven years they return to the United States for a visit. They're invited to stand before scores of congregations. Their leathery skin reflects a lifestyle that's a stark contrast to the air-conditioned comfort accepted by the audiences as normal.

The dedicated missionaries report with a sigh of relief that during their twenty-seven years out in the field, two Muslims finally accepted Jesus as Savior and Lord. They quote Henry Martyn, the nineteenth-century missionary, who toiled in prayer four hours every day: "I never expect to see a Muslim come to Christ."

The missionaries who gave their entire working lives to the promotion of the gospel were living examples of those who would live, even die for Christ. Now, I ask you, who would have the audacity to stand up and question the methods of this veteran missionary couple? Who among the congregations they visited would dare to suggest their approach could be altered and the results enlarged?

But that, precisely, is the question that should be asked today.

Investigation and Interaction

On my return to the United States, I talked with various leaders about the challenge of evangelism in non-Christian lands. I listened hard to what they had to say. Much to my amazement, I found the denominations and the parachurch organizations were not only without solid answers, they didn't even know what questions to ask. Their concept of training was this: Let a Christian leader from the West take the text of John 3:16 in one hand and the song "Jesus Loves Me" in the other and teach both to the lowest socioeconomic levels of the non-Western world.

While I applauded their dedication, I was convinced that their nineteenth-century methods fell short of current needs. These good and godly people were operating from a set of obsolete assumptions.

The people concerned with and involved with citizens of the Third World at the time could be divided into two groups:

1. Those committed to social service who believed that by improving living conditions through Christlike compassion, others would accept Christ;

2. Those who believed the rate of success of Third World evangelism was in direct proportion to the number of Western missionaries who crossed their borders.

Unfortunately, today neither way is really working. Yet Christian denominations continue to follow the same paths, and they are paralyzed through self-imposed limitations. Let me illustrate.

Experiments have been performed with predatory fish in which "attacking fish" are placed in a tank on one side of a glass divider. Other fish are put on the other side of the divider. The attacking fish propel themselves toward the other fish with vengeance—only to smash into the glass divider. Again and again they try. By the end of the day, they make no more attempts to attack.

The next morning the experimenters remove the glass partition. The attack fish now make no effort to destroy their natural prey. The fish have a self-imposed limitation so that

officers. In fact, these officers look to the Third World leaders for guidance and direction regarding their activities.

I refer to such organizations as World Vision, Evangelism Explosion, and Prison Fellowship International.

The West has a lot to share with the Third World, even as the Third World has a lot to share with the West. However, the moment we cross their borders, we go as guests, not as religious viceroys of a Western Church.

That's the only way it will work.

President Suharta, Republic of Indonesia; Col. Widya Latief, presidential secretary; John Haggai

Thomas "Tom" Stephens Haggai

8

We Must
Train Leaders

"The concept of reaching people of the Third World for Christ by training their own leaders is the most logical and effective approach to this tremendously important and gigantic problem."

E. L. BUICE

Mrs. Grace Sathyaraj of Bangalore, India, received training
at the first women's session in 1977. She now lectures on
"Doctrinal Overview"

The most effective means of making things happen is not to work among the poor or even the middle class. Success comes much faster when we work from the top down. National leaders—political, business, and church people—are those who make things happen.

Dr. John Sung

Dr. John Sung from China was used of God, I am convinced, to touch more lives across China, the Philippines, Indochina, Indonesia, Singapore, Malaysia, and Thailand than any one individual before or since.

Sung had earned his Ph.D. from Ohio State University. He was thoroughly trained theologically in the West. Even in the days of the Oriental Exclusion Act in the West, he was honored with an inundation of prestigious and high-paying opportunities in education and industry.

But in 1929, he returned to his native China. When he arrived at the South China Sea, he discarded his Western clothes and all of his Western honors—except his Ph.D.—and donned the blue-denim robe of the Chinese peasant.

87

As soon as he arrived at his father's house, the elder Sung advised: "Now that you are so highly educated, you can teach in a prestigious university and give your brothers a good education." But John Sung told his father that God had called him to evangelism.

John Sung died fifteen years later, but not until God had used him to change the spiritual complexion of that entire area of the world. He left Indonesia a legacy of 5,000 evangelistic teams with three members to a team.

Sung's ministry laid the base for the evangelical witness now in Singapore and parts of Malaysia. You can still see his influence in Indochina and mainland China. He literally molded for God the lives of many of Indonesia's most ardent patriots.

Sung was able to make great strides not only because he was a faith-filled man, but because his fellow countrymen recognized him as one of the most highly educated people of the land. Although he was never elected to an office, he was one of their most influential men. He was a leader and was not afraid to use that role to further the cause of Christ.

If only the Western Church could appreciate this. The percentage of the world where its foreign missionaries can go is rapidly and steadily shrinking. Doors to missionary work are closing—some abruptly, others more subtly. In some countries, once a foreign missionary goes home on furlough, he cannot reenter the country. Visas are not being renewed.

In the meantime, church denominations throughout the United States and Europe meet at conventions debating the "why" of foreign missions. What they ought to face is the penetrating question: "How?"

The sincerity and concern of these Western churches are unquestionably genuine, yet many of them have a serious blind spot. It's a blind spot that says, in effect, "This is the way we've always done it, and we must continue to do it the same way." More importantly—and perhaps more pathetically—it is a blind spot which develops in organizations that hold to the past and are unable or unwilling to consider the possibility God may be directing us to new, more effective approaches in world evangelization.

Two Centuries of Service

The modern Protestant missionary movement will celebrate its two hundredth anniversary in 1992. This movement began when William Carey challenged the hearts and spirits of European Protestant Christians to take the gospel to all nations. Offering himself as an example, he sailed for India.

Since that time, dedicated missionaries have followed his footsteps, walking the same routes, until they have worn a trench into the soil from which they never can get out.

What many of today's mission organizations fail to realize is that the conditions of the era of William Carey no longer exist. At one stage Western governments were in nearly total control of most of Africa, Asia, and Latin America. This is no longer the case.

Today, churches in the Third World are no longer waiting with bated breath for the "foreign missionary" to come with the gospel message. To the contrary, many nationals are embarrassed to admit they have missionaries residing and working in their areas.

The head of one of the largest evangelical groups in the Middle East—a highly trained theologian and a world-famous churchman—flew to the United States specifically to plead with heads of mission organizations not to allow their short-term missionaries, especially the students they send in summertime, to identify with the local people.

"Right now, seventeen of our people are in jail because they were identified with the visiting short-term missionaries," he told an assembled group. "You see, Americans sometimes don't understand that they can come, show their movies, pass out tracts, give testimonies, see fine results, and return home with great joy. They don't realize that in identifying with the local people they are jeopardizing the liberty and, in some cases, the lives of those people who are contacted by the authorities as soon as the foreigners leave. The only reason that some of these governments do not immediately step in is because they don't want to risk losing foreign aid, and they know that were they to interfere, the various congressmen and senators would intervene."

Then he turned to me and added, "I don't know who planted the idea in your mind, but the Haggai Institute concept is the one idea that is valid for our area, because it is national reaching national. The problem today is that 'the trouble with foreign missions is that they are foreign.'"

A multi-national businessman who has traveled extensively understood our concept of training national leaders for the effective spreading of the gospel. Our conversations with my brother Tom reinforced this man's conclusion that American business, particularly through the American Management Association, had for years sent its key executives to intensive seminars on management techniques. These trained men and women returned to their companies and passed on to their colleagues what they had learned.

This leadership training approach was obviously succeeding in business. Why wouldn't it work in the Church? Why couldn't some carefully selected Christian leaders from Third World countries be trained in intensive seminars on the "how" of evangelism, and then return to their own nations to train their countrymen?

Today an estimated three-fourths of the Third World's people live in countries that either bureaucratically discourage or openly prohibit foreign missionary efforts. Therefore, it seems imperative that qualified Christian national leaders carry on gospel work within these "closed" countries. These national Christians long to learn the most effective way to present Christ relevantly to their own people without compromise and without offense.

What We Do

Haggai Institute, then, neither plants churches, publishes Bibles, sponsors orphans, distributes food, organizes seminars on labor-management relations, nor underwrites specialized research in systematic theology.

We provide training for national leaders. *And it's not the sort of training where a superior imparts his knowledge to inferiors. Rather, the training consists of the study and interaction of the leader participants for whom the faculty member suggests the direction, shares his particular expertise, and serves as a catalyst for the study, interaction, and reports that derive from the session.*

This, in my opinion, is the only logical approach to foreign missions.

Others agree. E. L. Buice, Pastor Emeritus of Rehobeth Baptist Church, Atlanta, Georgia, says, "The concept of reaching people of the Third World for Christ by training their own leaders is the most logical and effective approach to this tremendously important and gigantic problem."

Leaders Are the Key

Haggai Institute brings together leaders of the highest caliber and commitment to study and interact under the catalytic guidance of a credentialed faculty. Note: I didn't say I was looking for theologians, philosophers, educators, or scholars. I want leaders.

Who exactly are these Christian leaders? They're lawyers, doctors, dentists, government officials, university presidents, professors, ministers of foreign affairs, high court justices, psychologists, multinational businessmen, architects, Bible translators, and clergymen—from archbishops to pastors and evangelists.

These are the people who have the greatest potential to influence the greatest number of people for Christ in their countries. Already proven leaders, these men and women have considerable influence with both Christians and non-Christians.

These leaders are trained by carefully screened faculty who include Christian scholars from the Third World and a few guest lecturers from the West who combine spiritual depth, scholastic qualifications, and significant achievement in the area of evangelism.

Some H. I. participants lack a college degree; others have earned doctorates. Each applicant is an avowed evangelical with impeccable leadership performance and potential.

It would be innocent ignorance at best, or fatuous arrogance at worst, for anyone eavesdropping on one of our Singapore sessions to think he has the quintessential understanding to tower over the participant leaders.

Our Alumni

Appearances often deceive. Had you been in Singapore in 1977, during one particular session, the leadership stature of the affable man in tongs and casual attire, with the relaxed smile, may have surprised you. He commands position and respect in both the Mideast and the West. He pastors one of the largest congregations in his part of the world. Simultaneously, he served as head of his denomination and president of a seminary. He's Asia's premier Christian writer; he has authored or translated two dozen major volumes. Any H. I. faculty member or, for that matter, world Christian leader, could sit with enlightenment and blessing at his feet.

Other H. I. graduates and faculty members include Grace Sathyaraj who, in Bangalore, heads up one of India's prestigious schools with a predominantly Muslim student body.

Another is Guilhermino Cunha, senior minister of the Presbyterian Cathedral in Rio de Janeiro. Few Christian leaders in this century have occupied so strategic a position as this Brazilian. The first Protestant to graduate from his nation's War College, he serves as a sometime professor of law. He's an appointed member of the committee to rewrite the Brazilian Constitution, and he's chairman of the committee to draft the preamble. His peers and parishioners agree he's a superb communicator.

There's Fr. Dr. Anthony D'Souza, S.J. This evangelical servant of God holds a doctorate from the Vatican, took part in Vatican II, serves as Rector of the Francis Xavier University of Bombay, and consistently turns out some of the finest books on leadership, management, and personal relations. He is a leader of international renown who enjoys impeccable credits, both sacred and secular.

Who could be so brash as to brag, paternalistically, "I'm going to teach these Third World participants at Haggai Institute how to successfully serve the Lord"?

From a modest beginning—19 trained in evangelism in 1969—God has multiplied the ministry so the Haggai Institute has trained more than 4,800 leaders from 96 nations and five continents. Our goal is to train 10,000—who will transmit their training to one million others—by the year 2000.

That sounds ambitious, I suppose. But when you surround yourself with positive, dynamic world leaders who take Christ's words seriously, somehow this sort of goal seems to be a natural part of living.

Haggai Institute Session 31, 1979—seated (on chairs) L-R:
Mr. Nene Ramientos, Mr. Ah Tua Teo, Rev. Doug Cozart,
Mr. Ken Anderson, Dr. Ernest H. Watson, John Haggai,
Dr. Won Sul Lee, Dr. Benjamin Moraes, Dr. Chandu Ray,
Dr. George Samuel, Bishop Essamuah

9

Results Must
Be Measured

*"The genius of the Haggai Institute concept is in its simplicity—
and the results speak for themselves."*

Dr. Michael Youssef

Historic 100th Training Session, Third Quarter, 1986

Theory alone is not enough. The acid test is the effectiveness of this work as measured by the number of people evangelized. Even the most enthusiastic supporter of a typical American or European church denomination must admit that former approaches to mission work have produced far less than significant results. Undisputed facts prove that the philosophy of the Haggai Institute works.

Don't soil your ears or pollute your vision by listening to the well-meaning but folly-laden charges of detractors. There are those who groan that we should work on discipling believers one-by-one—that a program designed to win the masses in non-Christian lands jeopardizes the impact and integrity of the work of God.

I pray God will straighten the thinking of these saints. May He deliver them from such spurious ideas as those implied in such statements as: "Oh, we don't want mushroom growth; we want solid growth."

I pray for these people who seem bound by a fear, bordering on paranoia, that too many may come to know Christ.

Have they not heard of the 3,000 souls saved in one day at

Pentecost? Or the 5,000 conversions at the one service mentioned in Acts 4? Or the two entire cities—Sharon and Lydda—that turned to Christ under the preaching of the apostle Peter? Or the 30,000 souls who turned to the Lord week after week under the anointed preaching of Dr. John Sung?

What about Seoul, Korea's Young Nak Church growing from 27 refugees to 65,000 members in 40 years? Or that city's Yoido Full Gospel Church growing from 5 to over 500,000 in 13 short years?

Rapid expansion of the Church does not mean superficial conversion of the members.

If we're to stop the galloping spiritual deficit, and if we're to simply keep pace with the population growth—to say nothing of making inroads on the current lost—we must increase the number of conversions by more than *one and a half million each week!*

Nationals Need Nationals

We at Haggai Institute believe this can be realized through nationals reaching their fellow nationals.

Our fellow Christians should stop at once this habit of playing games with their heads—expostulating, philosophizing, spiritualizing. What they say is a natural response, but we are children of the supernatural, having received the divine nature of which Peter talks in his second letter.

Yet some of our most severe critics insist the method of world evangelism employed since William Carey went to India in the 1790s is sacrosanct. True, they believe in the divine inspiration of the Holy Scriptures, but they behave in a way that could lead one to conclude they also pay allegiance to the divine inspiration of the traditional method of overseas evangelism.

At our training sessions in Singapore, Third World leaders reveal fresh methods of evangelism, methods we are convinced God is honoring. The message of the gospel is unchanging; the methods of presenting it are ever-changing.

In 1971, the senior associate pastor of the Young Nak Presbyterian Church of Seoul, Korea, told his fellow participants in Singapore about a 200-foot illuminated cross the Church had erected at the northern boundary of South Korea; 200,000 North Korean soldiers maintained guard there. They had to see the cross, since their assignment required them to look south across the 38th Parallel. And the North Korean Government changed the 200,000 border-patrol soldiers every four months. So, 600,000 soldiers from communist North Korea saw that cross every 12 months. They also heard the electronically amplified gospel message beamed north to this area.

An H. I. participant from Argentina heard the testimony. He couldn't duplicate that situation exactly, but the cross at the Korean border gave him an idea.

In one of his projects he brought together 160 Roman Catholic priests (including some bishops) and 40 Protestant pastors for a seminar on evangelism. This was a first in Latin America, where the relationship between Catholic and Protestant has not been on the friendliest terms.

Yet the response to that seminar was so positive and enthusiastic that participants have requested a repeat seminar to which others would be invited.

The news spread. Today, both Protestants and Catholics in Peru, Chile, Paraguay, and Uruguay have asked for similar seminars.

The leader who envisioned, organized, and directed this project said that his Singapore experience changed his entire ministry.

Quick Results

With most of our alumni, effective outreach begins immediately after graduation. One of the reasons for this instant zeal is that only Christian leaders, evangelistically minded, are accepted for training. In other words, they are the people who are already capable of leading their fellow nationals *before* they

set foot in our classroom. All we do is add fuel and direction to
that flaming passion.

And here's the real test of our training program. Every
Haggai Institute alumnus and alumna, on the average, shares
his or her training with *at least 100 others.* And those who are
reached meet with and instruct others . . . who meet and
instruct others . . . . The compounding factor blows your
mind.

As more training sessions are conducted, greater numbers
of qualified applicants will be sponsored and accepted into the
program. As a result, literally millions will hear the gospel for
the first time.

This approach "opens" to the message of Christ an increasing number of areas previously "closed" to traditional
missionary endeavors.

The stories presented here are but a sample of what H. I.
graduates are doing throughout the world. Even though our
operation is not yet 20 years old, our 4,800 alumni have docu-
mented proof they have trained over three-fourths of a million
fellow nationals through their classes and individual contacts.

The proof is in the pudding.

PART III

THE PROGRAM

Doug Cozart, H. I. Vice President for Third World Relations

The theories of John Haggai make sense—pure and simple. Why the traditional missionary organizations of the Church still fail to recognize this lies somewhere beyond the scope of reason.

The Westerner, who still lives and works within the four walls of his self-imposed missionary compound, continues to be confused and bewildered. After all, no one can question his loyalty. He's willing to die for the cross of Christ and for the people whom he has felt called to serve. Why, then, does he suffer such antagonism and persecution? Why don't the people respond to the good news of the gospel as they should?

The reason is obvious, once we look at it from the viewpoint of the nationals. People everywhere want to *know* what to do, but we don't like being *told* what to do—especially by outsiders. Otherwise, all foreign efforts are viewed as little more than cultural colonialism or idealized imperialism.

Many groups talk about leadership training for Third World nations, but they use Western personnel, Western methods, and Western-produced materials. They even compound the problem by imposing upon them a foreign model.

The same holds true with missions.

Because of the growing pride of nationalism in what used to be underdeveloped countries, the people of Argentina, Peru, Chile, Korea, and other nations rebel at the thought that they're dependent upon Western missionaries instructing them on how to survive in this modern world.

On top of this, when the gospel is taught and preached, the message has that "Made in America" label sewn securely on anything they use or say.

A Modern Prophet

John Haggai, in this respect, is a modern prophet. Not only does he preach the Word of God without compromise, but also, he is able to see beyond the obvious and apply new insights that those in power had never before considered.

At the same time, Haggai has been committed to the valuable contributions of the local church. In his own situation, he has remained a tithing member of his local congregation. He believes God ordained the local church to be His primary vehicle for executing His work in the world. He reminds donors to his Institute that their first obligation is to their home church. That appeal notwithstanding, not everyone is convinced he is serving the Church at large.

It was Ibsen who once wrote: "The bravest is he who stands alone." John Haggai has had to stand alone many times. Slings and arrows were tossed at him by those outside and inside the organized Church.

He not only survived, he prospered.

There were many reasons for the success of his program—tireless energy, a willingness to be apart from his wife and terminally ill child 50 percent of the time, fervent prayer, and a strong faith that this was what God wanted him to do.

But ideas, alone, mean nothing. Will these ideas work? If so, how?

Now that leaders were selected and educated, a systematic operation had to be set in motion. This included several things:

1. a sharp focus on realistic goals;
2. an acceptable site for training;
3. recruitment of the best possible faculty and staff;
4. selection of the most qualified candidates for advanced leadership;
5. enough funds to make it all work.

Conceptualizing the idea of the Haggai Institute required the insights of Solomon; convincing others to follow demanded the leadership of Moses; making it work took the energy of Samson.

John Haggai embodies all three.

JCM

Super Servant Seminar IV, Hawaii, July 1987

John Haggai with B. D. Jatti, Vice President of India,
22 November, 1974

10

The Operation Must
Have a Sharp Focus

"We aim not for the masses, rather for the select few who can give us the 'leading edge' in promoting the gospel of Jesus Christ."

JOHN HAGGAI

Rev. Kun Ho Choi, Session 31—this H. I. alumnus planted
100 new churches in India after returning from Singapore
training, and also quadrupled his own church in Korea.

Were many a fully trained missionary from a traditional American seminary to enter the H. I. program, he would be hopelessly lost. After one day, he would be convinced his seminary professors were speaking one language, and the H. I. faculty another.

In seminary, the young graduate learned how to teach, how to evangelize, and how to organize. He was also encouraged to use the things you can't teach—his faith and his genuine concern for people. But, with rare exception, even if he scored A+ in every one of his classes, he would still not be prepared to work with H. I. Our methods would be as foreign to him as are the nationals he's attempting to reach.

And that's the key. Just as the nationals are foreign to him, he is foreign to them. What he is speaks so loudly that sometimes the people cannot hear what he's saying.

Critics Abound

Because of the unique approach of the Haggai Institute, others have been quick to criticize our operation. Those who criticize do so, for the most part, from a background that's molded by traditional ways of evangelizing. We understand this. At the same time, we can look them all straight in the eye and justify our sharp focus in line with the fact that our operation meets real, not perceived, needs.

Some say, for instance, that we are "elitists," in that we center our attention on only the highest socioeconomic echelon in the Third World from which we select participants.

To this charge we plead "Guilty." We quickly admit we aim not for the masses, but rather for the select few who can give the "leading edge" in proclaiming the gospel of Jesus Christ to the masses. The H. I. alumni demonstrate proved leadership ability. If they have been successful in leading their countrymen in business, law, medicine, or any of the other secular disciplines, it makes sense these committed followers of Jesus Christ would also have the talent and ability to lead in spiritual matters as well.

Some say we are so small we can't make any real impact. One of the normal questions asked me is: "How many do you have at a session of Haggai Institute?" When I answer "Twenty-five," some turn up their noses and say, "Really? Just a few months ago we had over twelve thousand in one of our seminars."

I congratulate them. But to match their operations with ours is really comparing apples and oranges. Perhaps it's better to say it's like comparing the number of preschoolers to the number of people doing postdoctoral studies at prestigous universities in the West.

Our participants are handpicked leaders from among those who already have the expertise to make things happen in their nations and can multiply their work a hundredfold.

We are criticized for being uncooperative.

I suppose that, too, might be a justified observation. But there's a healthy reason for our stance. It is not the policy of the Haggai Institute to operate jointly with other Western organizations for two reasons:

1. To work jointly with other Western organizations discredits us with the national Third World leadership who object to Western methods for meeting their evangelism challenge. They perceive the Haggai Institute to be unique in our vision of nationals; they are aware we encourage leadership from among their own people to evangelize.

Many full-time missionaries know this and, taking us aside, clandestinely talk with us, expressing a longing that their boards would understand. Those who are on the firing line, so to speak, see the reality of things, while so often their boards, unfortunately, do not.

Some mission heads who have been away from the action for fifteen to twenty-five years have lost touch with demographics, social changes, and cultural attractions.

2. In the unstable political situations among Third World nations, and in the case of the coming to power of a government hostile to the Western world, not only are missionaries deported, but our national leaders could go to jail for their association with foreigners.

To the outsider, we are uncooperative. But those who know us realize we cooperate with all Third World Christian organizations who are genuinely Third World, and not simply fronts for Western or Soviet organizational ideologies and methodologies.

We cooperate, for example, with Eagles Evangelism—a major parachurch organization in Singapore. They have invited me to conduct some large rallies with them. Previously I've been happy to conduct large rallies; now I urge them to use their national evangelists.

We also cooperate with the methods of any legitimate indigenous Third World organization. Nonetheless, we cannot, in good conscience, continue to foster missionary methods that were valid a few generations ago, but no longer apply to today's situation.

With our unique focus, do we run the risk of being misunderstood? You bet. But, that's one of the risks we have to take in order to stand by our proved philosophy.

But let me ask this. Must we ignore the needs of three billion people who have yet to hear about Jesus, just to gain the support of a comparatively small coterie of Western believers in the mission apparatus, who look upon any innovative program as a threat to Christian unity? Who really are the elitists?

We are committed to seeing the job done. New situations require new methods. The message remains exactly the same; it's the same carried with the apostle Paul as he preached on Mars Hill; it's the same that William Carey took to India; it's the same that was uttered by John G. Patton in the South Seas, by Livingstone in Africa, by Henry Martyn in Asia, and all the other dedicated missionaries of the past.

We are accused of spurning the expertise of other missionaries. That's just not true. Some of our most ardent supporters in terms of prayer, financial contributions, and third-person influence are Western missionaries. Those who support us understand the program of H. I. and agree with it.

The leader of one of America's most effective and God-blessed parachurch organizations asked H. I. Vice President Doug Cozart, "What control does John Haggai have on the leaders when they return to their respective nations?"

His question shouted out the "big-daddyism" attitude of the interrogator.

Doug Cozart didn't budge one inch. Instead, he responded, "The same control that your seminary has had on you since you graduated."

Sound Assumptions

How do you communicate the gospel to a Soviet who speaks only Russian? You must speak Russian, of course. Any serious soul-winner assumes the importance of speaking a language easily understood by the audience—whether that audience be one or 1,000.

But language is only part of communicating. Meanings lie not in words, but in people. What we called "hot" fifty years ago, the young folks now call "cool."

Dr. Dawaskie, president emeritus of Gordon College, Rawalpindi, Pakistan, said, "You Americans love the word 'freedom'; our young people find it repugnant. They associate freedom with Western nudity and drunkenness. So when the American says, 'The truth shall make you free,' they cringe.

"We say, 'God can change your life; give your life to God.' The Hindu has millions of gods. He has a god for every conceivable area of life—a god for health . . . a god for wealth . . . a god for sex . . . a god for business . . . . When you refer to God as the Supreme Person, he's confused, because his god is not a person, and his god is not supreme. You must refer to Christ the Creator, showing that He is the Source of all life and that all life inheres in Him. That puts Him in their understanding above all their gods.

"If you refer to Jesus as the Son of God when you're dealing with a Muslim, he'll think, 'I have more respect for Jesus than that. He was a great prophet.' This Christian, like all Christians, blasphemes in his eyes. He believes that God is father, Mary is mother, and Jesus is a bastard child by their union. He'll turn you off as profane infidel.

"You say to the Buddhist, 'Come to Jesus; He'll give you eternal life.' The Buddhist responds in his heart, 'Doesn't the simpleton know that life is suffering and that the ultimate objective of life is nonexistence when my suffering will cease?'

"Do you catch the point? The essence of the gospel is changeless; the expression of that essence must be adapted to the mindset of the audience.

"You must begin where the *person* is, not where *you* are at the moment."

Our focus of operation is predicated on the assumption that nationals best reach other nationals. For Western foreigners to go into a country with the gospel of Jesus Christ can be, and has been, interpreted by godless leaders as an intrusion of foreign ideology.

One American organization, blessed of God and highly effective in the West, decided to send scores of young people into the Arabic-speaking countries for the purpose of securing names and addresses of the people. The follow-up stage of this plan was to write an evangelistic-type letter which would be translated into Arabic and mailed directly to those people contacted by the young Americans.

That made sense to traditional Western thinking. But it gave us at H. I. more than a little anxiety. Such a plan had obviously not been thought out in terms of the situation and needs of the Arabic-speaking people for several reasons:

1. Young girls soliciting names and addresses of people could get into trouble;

2. Young men asking females for their names and addresses could get into serious trouble;

3. The post offices would surely confiscate letters sent from the United States in large quantities;

4. The addressees of the letters could be put in serious jeopardy simply for receiving such mail.

Why would any denomination or parachurch group put its workers and its program in such peril? The only answer I can imagine is that men and women with more compassion and dedication than judgment, sit thousands of miles away and, while genuinely wanting to do the work for God, come up with ideas totally anachronous to the needs of the people.

While Haggai Institute does not compromise the gospel, it does realize its obligation to understand local needs.

When, pray tell, will the rest of Western Christendom wake up to that fact?

11

Finding an
Acceptable Site

*"The Haggai Institute trains indigenous Christians in Third
World Nations—sending them home to preach to their own
people—many of whom heretofore have shunned Christianity
as a 'white man's religion.'"*

PAUL HARVEY

John Haggai and newscaster Paul Harvey

While it is true that Haggai Institute has encountered more than its share of critics, others were mindful of the fact that our method of operation is the only reasonable approach to world-wide evangelism today.

Endorsements

Chuck Colson, former White House aide, now chairman of Prison Fellowship International, had climbed the mountain-top of success and plunged into the deepest pit of humiliation. Perhaps it's because he's seen the world from a variety of per-spectives that he is aware of what H. I. is all about and has become one of its solid supporters.

"John Haggai understands the Third World," he writes, "and is training its best minds to be Christian leaders. He understands world missions, and is equipping these leaders to establish indigenous ministries. I believe in John and am thrilled with the tremendous results I've seen in the lives of these national leaders."

Popular columnist and commentator Paul Harvey once

said, "The Haggai Institute trains indigenous Christians in Third World nations, sending them home to preach to their own people—many of whom heretofore have shunned Christianity as a 'white man's religion.'"

Both Chuck Colson and Paul Harvey clearly understand what H. I. is all about and what the Institute is doing. They realize leaders of the Third World can have a tremendous impact on their own people.

They, along with other supporters, have come face-to-face with some of our graduates. They are amazed at the success of people such as Aaron Mlenga, a clergyman from Malawi.

"Since I returned home from Haggai Institute," he says, "I have organized four different revival and training sessions. At Mkembe Village, we gathered 957. At Chilim'mimba Village, 1,079 attended. In Zozo Village we had 2,005. And we reached 2,017 in Bwanali Village.

"In all these meetings, I met separately with elders, deacons, women's union members and older mature Christians. I translated all my Haggai Institute materials into the local language, and shared with those established Christian leaders how they could best communicate the gospel to nonbelievers.

"After transferring the training to them, I sent them out in every direction to implement the training and evangelize the neighboring villages. The response was marvelous. On one Sunday following the training sessions, I preached, and 1,199 villagers came to receive Jesus Christ as their personal Savior."

Vera Vassilieff is a wife and mother of three children, associate professor in pharmacology, an internationally published researcher in the field of medicine, winner of national rewards for research, and an active member of her local church.

"I was very insecure about my personal role and responsibility in the leadership ministry which God has given me," she says. Yet in the first year following her H. I. training in Singapore, Dr. Vassilieff held a training seminar for 50 Sunday school teachers from churches in 5 cities around Sao Paulo. She shared her H. I. leadership training with 120 ministers and church elders at a Christian leadership conference. And she presented the program "Being a Leader" to over 400 adults, including people from many denominations and walks of life.

Attending Haggai Institute was just what she needed to gain much-needed confidence. "I prayed a lot about the issue," she says, "after having listened to teachers at the Institute. I realized in spite of my limitations, I could be comfortable being a leader."

Mr. Eden Lucksom is a teacher in India who has been extremely successful in his ministry through evangelism-training seminars. In a recent letter to me, Mr. Lucksom wrote: "Brother, I want to tell you one thing. Evangelism is very difficult here so close to the India/China border. Some of our alumni are going into areas like Nepal, Bhutan, and Sikkim where open preaching or proselytizing is against the law. In spite of all these hindrances, evangelism is making steady headway in these border kingdoms."

Aaron Mlenga, Vera Vassilieff, and Eden Lucksom are but three of the graduates of H. I. who utilize the techniques learned at Singapore and are able to return to their villages and neighboring lands and tell the people they meet about Jesus Christ.

Yet, none of this would have been possible had not a site been selected for training which would be acceptable to people from the Third World.

Choosing the Site

While we are right on target when we suggest that the best possible teachers for Third World nationals are fellow citizens from these countries, we would undermine all we attempted to do if the leaders were forced to attend sessions in the continental United States or within the borders of some other established Western nation. Although the returning leader would attempt to maintain his identity with his people, his image, at best, would be tarnished because of his direct exposure to Western schools and philosophy.

The only way around this would be to select a site in an area free of political controversy.

Switzerland seemed to be the most natural place. After all, wasn't the name Switzerland synonymous with neutrality and internationalism? Was it not the headquarters for the international Y.M.C.A. and the International Red Cross?

Several attempts at finding a permanent location in Switzerland failed. As explained earlier, we lost a lot of valuable time and an abundance of money, partly because some trusted businessmen backed out of deals at the last minute.

Just about that time, in early 1969, Dr. Bob Pierce told us of a three-story chalet in the tiny village of Istlewald, near Zurich. "You can buy this from a man who has run out of funds," he promised. To me, this was confirmation we should hold our classes in Switzerland for our international program.

Another session was held in Switzerland in 1970. Although the concept was evidently valid and was working as predicted, doubts began to arise concerning the location. Switzerland was ideally neutral, but there were unsettling problems. The weather provided an abrupt change from Third World conditions. And as hard as the Swiss cooks tried, they couldn't seem to present an acceptable diet for stomachs used to rice and Oriental flavorings. Even though the people spent most of their time interacting with each other in study and discussions, they were surrounded by a culture and an environment to which they were unaccustomed.

I began an active search for another location. We had the right concept in mind; the logic made sense. But unless we found a suitable "home" for the sessions, all our work would be in vain.

In spite of our earlier setbacks, we pressed forward.

Seven factors guided our decision for a site location:

1. The specialized studies would be conducted in a neutral country so that the graduates would not wear a "Made in U.S.A." label.

2. The emphasis would be on the "how" of evangelism.

3. The faculty would be drawn predominantly from Third World Leaders.

4. The student-faculty ratio would be kept low; there would be no mass production.

5. Attendees would have to be screened carefully, not only by the Haggai Institute leadership, but also by their peers.

6. The language of instruction would be English—the one language common to all the faculty members and to a host of top leaders in the Third World.

7. Each applicant would be expected to pay a percentage of the cost of his or her training. The training would not be handed out free—but must be sought after and worked for.

It's easy to see that to meet all these criteria, a neutral site for education was a must. By the grace of God, we settled on the ideal location. Today, the Haggai Institute training center is strategically located in Singapore—the crossroads of the Orient. This great city-state is situated within 3,000 miles of half the world's population. And because Singapore is both independent and neutral, people from all nations can meet on ground free of domination by either the West or the Communists.

Why is this so significant? Simply because a person from any Third World country can come to Singapore and return home with no suspicion he has been influenced by "foreign" ideology. Haggai Institute alumni must not be perceived as spokesmen for "alien interests."

Through the tireless effort of many, plus the generous contributions of others, a center was selected and purchased.

Today, the Cecil B. Day Center reflects the Haggai Institute's professional approach to instruction. I've often advised young clergymen: "Don't be too specific in your prayers by telling God what *you* want; you just might get more than you ever dreamed or deserved."

The Cecil B. Day Center is one example of what I'm talking about.

Deen and Cecil B. Day, Sr., whose contributions enabled H.I. to obtain the Singapore property and for whom the training center is named

12

Recruiting the
Best Staff

"Evangelizing leadership development for evangelism, church growth, and lay involvement, Haggai Institute has pioneered in training nationals from many lands for indigenous as well as cross-cultural ministries. Both its program and international teaching staff have enjoyed well-deserved recognition."

CARL F. H. HENRY

Michael Youssef, Ph.D.

The concept was in place. An ideal site had been selected. But like every other academic endeavor, you can have the finest buildings in the world, up-to-date equipment, and plush surroundings, but without a trained, dedicated staff, your program is worthless.

The Significant Difference

What, for example, keeps Harvard, Yale, Oxford, Cambridge, and similar institutions of higher learning as models with which others are compared? Certainly the criteria do not include buildings; some facilities are old and outdated. It's not the modern equipment that separates these schools from others; most of today's colleges and universities are filled with state-of-the-art computers and other aids to education. Instead, the one dimension that has made and keeps them as ideal centers of learning is the top-notch faculty, many of whom have earned reputations as giants in their fields.

I was determined to ensure that those who enrolled in our leadership seminars would be led by people who possessed not only a solid faith and a strong evangelical outlook, but also whose credentials would measure up to any of those who taught at a prestigious university.

I told other people—some of whom were among the recognized leaders and spokespeople for the Church—about the H. I. concept of bringing world leaders together to prepare to evangelize their own.

Dr. Han Kyung Chik

Dr. Han Kyung Chik, pastor emeritus of the world's largest Presbyterian Church—in Seoul—was an enthusiastic backer and professor. Even though he had reached retirement age; pastored a congregation of 20,000 (1969, now 65,000); served on scores of boards; headed orphanage movements, schools, programs for the elderly and disadvantaged; presided over dawn prayer meetings; preached on all six continents; and led in the establishment of hundreds of churches in Korea and around the world, Dr. Han carved out the time to serve as our respected senior faculty member from the first session.

Our invalid son Johnny was so impressed with Dr. Han that every time his name was mentioned, Johnny's face wreathed in smiles. His favorite article of clothing was a sweater that Dr. Han gave him. Johnny was proud of that sweater and wore it with great enthusiasm.

Dr. Won Sul Lee

One of these modern-day leaders is among the world's most influential academicians—Dr. Won Sul Lee, who at the time I met him was dean of the Graduate School of Korea's Kyung Hee University and secretary general of the International Association of University Presidents, and is now president of Han Nam University in Taejon, Korea. Dr. Lee, who earned his Ph.D. in American History from Case Western Reserve, is a rare individual who has the best of Western academic credentials, while maintaining a solid identity with people of the Third World. On top of this, he is a dedicated Christian who loves his Lord and the Church.

In my way of thinking, Dr. Lee would be the ideal person to serve as faculty chairman. I knew he was an extremely busy person whose schedule was jam-packed with obligations to his institution and government. Others, I supposed, might criticize me for even daring to ask a man of his caliber to join our ranks. But I've never been accused of being shy. I'm a firm believer in asking for something you really need. So, I asked.

Without a second's hesitation, Dr. Lee said, "I'd be honored to help you in any way possible."

Do you see what I mean about asking?

Dr. Lee served in this position until 1981.

Dr. Chandu Ray

I met Dr. Chandu Ray in the late sixties. He was a handsome Pakistani whose presence projected an aura of gracious authority and scintillating brilliance. He cut quite a figure in his bishop's habit.

Chandu Ray, who came from a wealthy Pakistani family, wandered from one religion to another for twenty-seven years trying to find an answer to his deepest questions and needs. By his own testimony, he came to know the Lord at the age of twenty-seven while visiting a friend who was preparing to go to the hospital for surgery.

At the time I got to know Chandu Ray, he was the head of "COFAE"—the Coordinating Office for Asian Evangelism—located in Singapore.

Dr. Ray was well received when he led some sessions at our seminar in 1971. He stressed that the Christian ought to find points of agreement in establishing contact with people of other faiths. Above all, he urged, Christians ought to demonstrate a spirit of true love so their interactions with these people would not be confrontational, but gracious and gentle. It was his view that too often Christians who are ignorant of these philosophies and religions approach Third World people with all the warmth and charm of a stopped-up sink.

After a couple of years as guest lecturer, he joined H. I. as head of the Singapore office and as faculty anchorman for the international sessions in Singapore.

Dr. Ernest Watson

I had heard of Dr. Ernest Watson of Australia in 1953 from Dr. Ralph Mitchell, a British clergyman who predicted the two of us would "hit it off." Fourteen years later, when I had opportunity to meet and share breakfast with Dr. Watson, that prediction came true.

On Watson's first visit to Indonesia, he was so moved by the openness of the people to hear about Jesus Christ, he determined to do whatever he could in the future to help them. While he had preached and become acquainted with people in many parts of the globe, the citizens of the Third World captured his heart.

Dr. Watson had pastored some influential churches in Australia and was a pioneer in religious radio and television broadcasting. His birth to British parents could have marked him as a white Westerner, but his rearing and ministry placed him squarely in the Eastern Hemisphere. Consequently, he was as free from a colonial mentality as any white Westerner I have ever known.

My feeling was echoed by an international leader whom I respected. "You ought to enlist Dr. Watson," he said. "He's a Baptist, but he's bigger than any denomination; he's an Australian, but his influence extends around the world."

Late in September 1969, I asked Dr. Watson if he would serve as dean. He agreed. Now, it's something for a man sixty-five years of age to identify himself with an untried, highly criticized concept that could tarnish his long-standing reputation for good judgment. But he took his stand, and for six years Dr. Watson literally held the seminars together.

Arriving early to greet the leaders, he attended every

session. He handled numerous logistical details and monitored all extracurricular activities.

One Anglican Bishop serving in Singapore perhaps said it best: "The Haggai Institute, which many people around the world today identify as the 'second stage of the world evangelism rocket,' would never have become a reality had it not been for the selfless devotion of Dr. Watson to the command of Christ and to the highest welfare of people living in the Third World."

I couldn't agree more.

The Latin America Connection

Haggai Institute's involvement with Latin America is the result of a remarkable chain of events. Dr. Bill Hinson was the first Baptist pastor to include H. I. in his congregation budget. Bill and his wife Betty introduced me to Mr. Tom Cundy, who made it possible for me to meet with representatives of the Maclellan Foundation of Chattanooga, Tennessee. After the trustees of the Foundation heard the H. I. presentation, they sent the Foundation lawyer, the late Jere Tipton, to Singapore to evaluate the program. What he saw he liked, and he endorsed the Haggai Institute concept. The Foundation since then has told others about the work and supported H. I. through gifts.

The Foundation's president—Mr. Hugh O. Maclellan, Sr.—introduced me to the Rev. Bill Mosely, a Presbyterian missionary to Brazil, and to Dr. Benjamin Moraes, a Brazilian Christian statesman.

Rev. Mosely asked why we didn't include Latin America in our program. Dr. Moraes pressed me to move into Brazil.

I hadn't considered Latin America a priority. After all, Latin America had the Bible; most Asians did not.

A few months later, on my arrival in Singapore for a session, Dean Watson told me, "Dr. Moraes is in Japan, and he's taking an eight-hour flight here just to talk with you about including Latin America in the H. I. program."

Dr. Moraes met me the next day. He was persuasive. I was awed by this man who could read, write, and speak twelve languages; who had written the penal code for Brazil; who had served as a cabinet minister on three different occasions; who had built the Copacabana Presbyterian Temple into a world-renowned church; who had written forty books; and taught law at the University of Rio de Janeiro.

With eyes riveting me, he argued his case. "You must understand," he insisted, "that the gospel of Jesus Christ is not reaching those who will make the decisions for Brazil. We thank God for the missionaries, but they are either working with Indians in the mountains, doing translation work, or heading some vocational activity in the cities. No one is doing for Brazil what Haggai Institute is doing for the East."

The H. I. leadership endorsed his appeal. The first Brazilian participant was the Rev. Guilhermino Cunha, senior associate pastor of the Copacabana Church and present pastor of Rio's Presbyterian Cathedral. Since Dr. Moraes' death, Cunha has taken a place on the H. I. faculty.

Today, Abrahao da Silva serves as executive director of Haggai Institute (Latin America) and Guilhermino Cunha serves as chairman of the H. I. (Latin America) Board.

Singapore Leaders

During the early seventies, a young Singapore clergyman worked with us for a short time. I am indebted to him for introducing me to Solicitor Lai Kew Chai (now the respected Mr. Justice Lai Kew Chai of the High Court in Singapore).

At that time, there was speculation that Singapore might be forced to restrict the space available to organizations headquartered in the West. They were very likely to be restrained in carrying out their dreams and plans from Singapore. After all, Singapore can't house everybody who wants residence there. About 2.5 million live on that delightful little island nation of less than 275 square miles. However, since we were a Third

World organization, with a Third World faculty, Third World participants, Third World curriculum, and since all the participant selection, curriculum determination, and program execution were being done in the Third World by Third World people, it seemed entirely logical that we seek Third World organizational status. In fact, it would be preferable. If the leaders coming for the seminars were to go back as the product of an American effort—if, in effect, they went back with a "Made in America" label on their back—it would disfranchise them with their own people.

As I was pondering this and praying about it in my study one night, I felt a compulsion to go to Singapore and see what could be done about accomplishing this objective. I called my Board members. I said, "I feel a compulsion to fly to Singapore," and I told them the reason.

"Well, go ahead," they said. "We're certainly not going to stand in the way."

"But it's going to cost about $1,800, and I have no evidence that it will achieve what I desire." They graciously insisted that I must go ahead. I didn't have the heart to tell them that we didn't have the money for the project, so I raised a personal loan to get there and back.

In Singapore the young clergyman said, "I want you to meet a brilliant solicitor with Lee and Lee, Singapore's most prestigious law firm." He introduced me to a handsome, thirty-one-year-old Malaysian-born Chinese Singaporean, who at that early age had already distinguished himself as a skilled solicitor.

The solicitor listened to my proposition, understood exactly the desire, gave obvious evidence of his commitment to world evangelism and said he would proceed with the steps needed to achieve the objective. In less than thirty hours I was on a plane back to the United States. The Haggai Institute was incorporated as Haggai Institute for Advanced Leadership Training Ltd., Pte. It became a Singapore corporation under the Singapore Companies Act with Singapore directors.

To my dying day, I will applaud the far-visioned, New Testament-type expansiveness of spirit that gave to the American Board the grace to release a measure of control. They have that rare humility that is willing to support what it cannot dominate.

On the other hand, I applaud the Singapore Directors for their willingness to put their reputations at risk in taking on the awesome responsibility of a fledgling Christian organization.

Canon Yip Tung Shan, a Singapore shipping magnate, who entered the Anglican priesthood in later life, serves as chairman of the Singapore board and trustee of the international board.

I first met Canon Yip when I was speaking at Singapore's St. Andrew's Cathedral, and he was taking part in officiating at the service. I did not know at the time he was father of the young lady married to the young solicitor, Lai Kew Chai.

Only their insistence on no recognition prevents me from telling the thrilling story of the enormous support of these quiet H. I. (Singapore) leaders.

Other Leaders

Among the graduates and leaders of the H. I. program are some of the world's significant publishers, writers, and journalists. That's important, for unlike the United States, television is not as pervasive in the Third World. For literate people, books are the most influential medium for mass communication.

Bedan Mbuga is one example. Mbuga was a pharmaceutical salesman from Kenya when he came to Singapore. During his time in Singapore, he was smitten by the conviction he must get into publication in order to extend the witness of the Christian gospel. He took over a magazine called *Step,* raised funds, secured facilities, and upgraded equipment. Within two years, *Step* outsold *Time* and *Newsweek* in five African nations, including Nigeria—Africa's largest nation.

Later, Bedan launched a second magazine: *Beyond.*

Willie Marguez of Manila, one of the lecturers at H. I., instructs in writing and publishes *Omni* which, at last report, has a greater distribution than any American or British magazine in the Philippines.

The Rev. Richard Bowie, an Australian citizen of Indian origin, left a promising secular career in patent law to pursue theological studies. He served widely as a pastor, teacher, and administrator in India, Great Britain, Israel and Australia. From 1970 to 1974 he was principal of Bishop's Anglican Theological College in Calcutta. He is the author of books and theological papers. Since 1975, Richard has taught at H. I. and now holds the title: Director of training.

Richard's wife, Audrey, was born in India. In her lectures to women's sessions at H. I., her sensitive handling of delicate issues for Third World women results in the cutting away of unscriptural cultural chains for many and the revealing of the Christian woman and her service as Christ sees her.

Dr. George Samuel, dean of H. I., has earned degrees both sacred (Master's from Fuller Theological Seminary) and secular (Doctorate in Nuclear Medicine from the University of California). He has worked as an acclaimed research scientist for the Government of India and as a consultant to the United Nations. He serves also on the boards of several international Christian organizations. Whenever he addresses participants at an H. I. seminar, he is regarded as one of its favorite instructors.

Although Doug Cozart was born and educated in the United States (University of Arizona), he spent most of his adult life in the Third World. Cozart formerly served with Dr. Bob Pierce as director of the embryonic World Vision program in Viet Nam where he supervised the burgeoning ministry of relief, education, and evangelism that touched thousands of Vietnamese lives through the Evangelical Church.

Doug, who is now with H. I., serves as its Vice President of Third World Relations.

To augment the regular instruction schedule, each training session features at least one guest lecturer who is particularly skilled in some specific aspect of evangelism and communications. Among those who have been included on our roster of guest lecturers are:

- Mr. Ken Anderson, president of Ken Anderson Films, who has traveled for H. I. at his own expense, donated materials, and taught alumni how to use audiovisual equipment in lands where there is no electricity;
- Dr. Carl Henry, founding editor of *Christianity Today* magazine;
- Dr. Robert Walker, editor, *Christian Life* magazine;
- Dr. G. L. Johnson, Senior Minister of the People's Church, Fresno, California;
- Dr. Reg Klimionok, Senior Minister, Garden City Christian Church, Brisbane, Australia;
- Dr. Paul Meyer, Founder of "Success Motivation Institute";
- The Most Rev. D. W. B. Robinson, Anglican Archbishop of Sydney, Australia;
- Dr. E. Eugene Williams, general director, American Missionary Fellowship.

Dr. Michael Youssef

In September 1975 I met a young man who would positively influence the future of H. I. I was in Sydney, Australia, for a major presentation about the Institute, when, unexpectedly, Michael Youssef came into my life.

A couple were unable to attend the dinner due to an unavoidable conflict. "There's an Anglican curate next door," said the couple, "who might be interested. In fact, he's an Egyptian, so he might find some special camaraderie in meeting Dr. Haggai."

During the after-dinner presentation, the twenty-six-year-old clergyman grasped the H. I. concept within the first few minutes. In my occasional glances at his table, I could tell that the lights in his mind were becoming brighter. Before the evening was over, Michael said to the entire group, "Now that's the answer to world evangelism today—national reaching national. The day of the Western White dominating the Christian ministry in non-Western lands is over."

Michael was a quick study. His enthusiasm did not stop with the serving of dessert. He arranged for me to present the H. I. concept before the largest Anglican Church in Australia and to speak at Moore College, his alma mater, and the University of Sydney.

Michael and I became instant friends. He was a man with the rare combination of youth and wisdom. I knew he would be an asset to our program. After several one-on-one conferences and some urging by others on our staff, Michael joined our program in 1977 on a part-time basis. One year later he moved to Atlanta and was made Vice President. He rose up the ladder until he assumed the responsibility as Chief Operations Officer, worldwide.

God used Michael to organize and lead the Mideast seminars which began in 1979 and have continued to this day. He is recognized as an authority on Islam. It is my view that he and his colleagues from the Arabic-speaking nations have done more to introduce some key leaders in Islamic nations to the true meaning of the gospel of Christ than any other group at work today.

Dr. Youssef, who earned his doctorate at Emory University, reluctantly left full-time work at H. I. in 1987. He now serves as Rector of Atlanta's newly formed Church of the Apostles—an evangelical church in the Anglican/Episcopal tradition. He continues his H. I. involvement—overseeing finances, advising on strategy, writing materials, lecturing at Singapore, and serving as an officer of the corporation.

These are just some of the dedicated servants of God who have given of their time and talents to teach and serve at the

Haggai Institute. Because of their devotion and tireless work, respected theologian and author (and one of our guest lecturers) Carl F. H. Henry said, "Emphasizing leadership development for evangelism, church growth, and lay involvement, Haggai Institute has pioneered in training nationals from many lands for indigenous as well as cross-cultural ministries. Both its program and international teaching staff have enjoyed well-deserved recognition."

I have observed that you can put all high achievers into two classes: Those who are motivated to achieve to enhance their own personal images and achieve their own personal goals, and those who are motivated to achieve in order to help others meet their real needs.

The former, of course, greatly outnumbers the latter; it's unnatural to "in honor prefer one another." I have watched with amazement some of the world's great contemporary achievers as they exerted superhuman effort and demonstrated an uncanny insight to achieve recognition by position or through enormous wealth. But I have gazed with reverential awe and unspeakable admiration at the Dr. Watsons, the Dr. Hans, and men and women like them who have invested their enormous talents and energies into the lives of people and nations who could not promise them wealth, or power, or status.

But that's the sort of people we've had on the H. I. staff.

May God bless them all.

13

Private Funding Is
the Only Way

"I have never in my life met anyone who can challenge someone to open his pocketbook for a worthy cause better than my brother, John. Perhaps his success is due to the fact that he believes so strongly the Great Commission—and gives sacrificially himself."

DR. TOM HAGGAI

John Haggai in deep discussion with Trustee John Bolten

The Haggai Institute cannot be entrapped by the now archaic methods of traditional missions. Nor dare it be identified with any government—Western or Eastern. Instead, the financial support for H. I. comes solely from private funding by devoted individuals, churches, businesses, and foundations who understand and appreciate the efforts of H. I. The continued generosity of our loyal supporters has enabled our staff to turn ideals into a first-rate operation.

Not the Masses

When I talk about private funding, I am not referring to the masses, but to carefully selected individuals, many of whom have been blessed by God with both individual success and personal wealth.

It would be preferable, humanly speaking, to have one million people giving $5.00 a year than to have a handful of people underwriting the total budget requirements. The reason is simple: If we lose one of the former, it doesn't make such a hole in the support net as it would were we to lose one of the latter. But I believe that H. I. benefits far more by identifying those select individuals who can give us the "leading edge" through their participation in the advancement of the gospel of Jesus Christ.

Henry F. McCamish, Jr., successful Atlanta insurance executive, was one of my "guardian angels" during the early days of H. I. It was he who arranged a healthy insurance program for me so that in the event of my untimely death, Chris and young Johnny would be protected. (Johnny died 14 February 1975.)

Hank did not believe in committees; he believed that if you wanted a job done, you handed it over to a capable person and let him go. Hank also did not like to work with the masses. He liked to focus on one person.

In 1976, he arranged for me to have lunch with Mr. James P. Poole, an insurance colleague. Since that day, Mr. Poole has been deeply involved with H. I., has taken several world journeys with me, and has served as Chairman of the Board of Trustees.

Hank McCamish convinced me by his performance that you can have "many" without having "much." You don't need a large number of the right kind of people to shoulder a great undertaking.

Think of a great choral conductor. He could be accused of exclusivity in that he will not permit monotones or even fair-to-middling singers in his professional chorale. He goes, instead, for top voices. We at H. I. are forced to go for people capable of giving, just as the maestro is forced to go with the people who are capable of singing. Frankly, we just don't have time to fill the mailbox with five-dollar bills secured by eyeball-to-eyeball contacts. And, we can't "mass market" the program.

Most of our support is raised this way—person to person. In nearly every instance, face-to-face discussion accomplishes what nobody can accomplish by cable, Telex, mail, telephone, or any other kind of nonpersonal communication. That is why I am on the road so much. I speak at conventions; some of our supporters introduce me to friends; they inform me about others; I fly to meet with them. Last year, I averaged nearly 1,000 flying miles a day. But it's been worth every bit of the time and effort. The results have been far more than I had ever imagined.

J. I. McCormick

In 1962 J. I. McCormick gave me a check for $7,000 with this explanation. "John, Opal (his wife) and I decided this year to do something a little different on our wedding anniversary. Instead of giving each other a gift, we're giving a combined gift, and we're giving it to you for your ministry."

It was with this gift that we incorporated and started the not-for-profit organization now known as Haggai Institute. For twenty-five years the McCormicks have supported this ministry with their prayers, their money, and their third-person influence. It was at a Sunday dinner, after I had preached in Birmingham, that the McCormicks brought some friends to meet me and hear more about H. I. One of those friends was the young man who now serves H. I. as chairman of the international board, Tommy Hill.

This philosophy has served me from the start. Carl Newton is a good example.

Carl Newton

Carl Newton is a Christ-centered executive, chairman and C.E.O. of Fox Photo, Inc.—the film service organization that has outlets throughout the world. Carl believes in the H. I. concept. He and his wife, Janie, are two of the dearest people you could ever hope to meet. When I met Carl in 1957, he had accompanied my visitation associate in soul-winning ministries. Carl was an enthusiastic supporter of the H. I. philosophy, but had never been what you would call a major financial contributor to the program.

Our first training session was scheduled for 15 September to 24 October 1969. This five-week session would cost us

$100,000. However, we had one slight problem. We didn't have the $100,000.

Two weeks earlier, at two o'clock in the afternoon, my secretary told me, "If we don't have the money by nine o'clock tomorrow morning, the entire training program will be canceled. The airlines will not wait any longer for payment on tickets; and other expenses are overdue." She then paused for a second and asked, "Dr. Haggai, why does God permit things like this?"

"Why?" is a natural question, but one which I dared not ask. I never blamed God. I blamed myself. Possibly I misunderstood the leading of the Lord. I headed for my office to pray that God would forgive me and give me guidance to know how to resolve this situation.

Before closing my door, I directed my secretary, "Please take down this cablegram message:

'Due to unexpected and unavoidable obstacles, training session postponed indefinitely. Regrets, regards, prayers.

Haggai.'"

Then, I added, for reasons I couldn't describe, "Don't send this cablegram out until four o'clock. If you don't hear from me by then, send it out."

I went into my office and closed the door. I "spread-eagled" on the floor, with my face buried in the carpet, crying to God to show me what to do to save what could be salvaged and bring a minimum reproach to His name. I asked Him to forgive me wherein I had gone ahead of Him.

I prayed without stopping for one and three-quarter hours.

"Dr. Haggai," my secretary called over the intercom.

The call was soft, but I heard it.

"Yes, what is it?" I barked, with a strain in my voice that showed my impatience.

"Carl Newton of San Antonio is on the line."

"I'm sorry. I can't talk with him now. I'll call him back," I said.

"But you *must* talk with him," she insisted.

"I don't have to talk with him or anyone else right now," I said. "Not even if it's the archangel Gabriel. I'm talking to his Boss."

But she persisted. Although I was annoyed at her, I took the call.

"Hi, Carl. How can I help you?"

"John," he said, "the market has gone to pot. My stock has dropped from $57 a share to $13 a share since May."

I had been straining my ears all day for encouraging news like that! "I'm sorry, Carl," I said. "I've been talking to the Lord about another matter, and I'll include the problem in my prayers."

"Wait a minute, knucklehead. You need some money, don't you?"

"Of course, but you don't sound as if you're in a position to help."

"Well, John, I can't give you any stock. Since I'm C.E.O. and a major stockholder, the divestiture of any stock by me could cause a run on the company."

"I understand, Carl."

"But wait a minute. We're able to get an eight percent, $100,000 loan for twelve months. Within this time I should be able to arrange for some liquidity. Call the man at your bank in Atlanta. Janie and I wired a gift of $100,000 a couple of hours ago."

I could scarcely believe what I had just heard. When I hung up the phone, the clock on my desk read six minutes before four. Fifteen minutes later, there would have been no Haggai Institute!

Later, Carl said to me, "I didn't know how I was going to do it, but I was impelled to act. I've never made a commitment I was proud of, which, at the time, I could see any possibility of fulfilling."

Many others among our donors understand exactly what he meant.

My brother Tom, whom I consider to be one of America's geniuses in business (he's chairman of the board of the I.G.A. chain) and in community service (he was the youngest man in history to be given the Silver Buffalo Award by the Boy Scouts of America), once announced to a large audience, "I have never in my life met anyone who can challenge someone to open his pocketbook for a worthy cause better than my brother, John. Perhaps his success is due to the fact that he believes so strongly the Great Commission—and gives sacrificially himself."

I guess that's how some people see me. If so, I'm really humbled. In fact, brother Tom was being kind. He, as well as anyone else who knows me well, realizes that asking for money does not come easy to me. Before I meet with any potential donor, I pray and "psyche myself up" to meet the challenge. Nonetheless, once that is done, I will ask for money boldly.

Shortly after the 15 August 1971 announcement by President Nixon in which he cut the dollar loose from gold and let it float, I realized we were in deep financial trouble. For one thing, where one dollar had purchased 3.33 Singapore dollars; it now purchased only 2.40. Commitments had been made in good faith that would cost us far more to fulfill than we understood at the time those commitments were made.

Cecil Day

I called Jim Frame, now a businessman in Dallas who serves on the H. I. Board but who was then my associate.

"Jim, give me the name of somebody in Atlanta who has money, will admit it, can make a decision, and can make it instantly. I want somebody who is not going to 'blow a lot of smoke,' like telling me, 'I must pray about it for thirty days,' or 'I've got to discuss this with my family,' or 'My board doesn't meet for four weeks and I must ask them.' Tell me somebody who can make a decision . . . now."

"Cecil Day," was Jim's immediate response.

"Who in the world is Cecil Day?"

"He's the one building that motel at . . . ."

"Oh, yes. The one at Clairmont and I-85. The budget luxury motel."

"That's right," said Jim. "He's the guy."

I got on the telephone and was put through to Cecil Day. "Mr. Day," I said, "I know you're a busy man, and so am I. Therefore, I'm not going to take a lot of your time. In order to get to the point quickly, I'd like to come over to see you right now. I have an important matter. I'll walk out of your office in exactly ten minutes by the clock."

"What do you want to see me about?" he asked.

"Money."

"How much?"

"Oh, come on, Mr. Day," I said. "You know that no one gives away interview information when he's setting up an appointment."

He chuckled.

"And furthermore," I said, "I am bringing some smelling salts in my left hand and some camphor in my right hand to revive you when you pass out after hearing how much I'm asking for."

"Come on," he insisted. "I'm looking forward to seeing you."

When I walked into his office, this tall, handsome, thirty-six-year-old man flashed that inimitable smile and said, "You don't remember me, do you?" Now, that can really disintegrate the morale of a fund-raiser when he realizes how badly he has prepared himself.

"No, I'm embarrassed. I really don't," I confessed.

"Seven years ago you conducted a meeting at the Mount Vernon Baptist Church of Atlanta. I was amazed that you had offered a hundred-dollar, hand-tooled family Bible to the person who would bring the largest number of people to the concluding Sunday night service. You told them that the number they brought had to be over the qualifying number of twenty-five. I was surprised, first of all, that you could get by with that in a church like Mount Vernon, and I was intrigued that you put a floor of twenty-five under the challenge."

"When you have studied the heroic proportions of my profile," I laughed, "you'll know that I'm not about to give a hundred-dollar, hand-tooled Bible to someone who brings only his next-door neighbor."

Cecil reminded me that his brother, Lon, had won the Bible by bringing forty-two people. Among those forty-two were Cecil, his wife Deen, and his five children. Then it all flashed before me, and I remembered the entire episode.

Then he turned to me and asked, "How much do you want?"

"Thirty-four thousand seven hundred dollars," I said. "Will you write me out a check, please?"

"No, I won't."

I looked at my watch, then looked at him and said, "Well, you have just saved yourself seven minutes. Thank you for seeing me. I've got to go."

"Where are you going?" he asked.

"To raise that thirty-four thousand seven hundred dollars," I replied.

"I'll give you five thousand dollars. But I won't give it to you all at once. I'll write you four post-dated checks for one thousand two hundred and fifty dollars each. Will that do it?" he asked.

"No, it won't do it, but it will help. Especially if you make a photocopy of the checks."

He looked a bit stunned. "What's this hangup you have on photocopying checks?"

"Oh, it's predicated on a sound biblical principle: 'Provoke one another unto good works.' I want others to see what you have done, and it may stimulate them to get their minds out of the hundred-dollar range. You see, I intend to go to people who have money and challenge them to give largely."

Cecil Day agreed to my proposal. And that was the beginning of one of the most incredible odysseys of stewardship that

I have had the privilege to observe.

From that initial gift came office space in his new building (to which Christine, my wife, had alerted him), the donation of what is now known as the Day Center—home of the International Training Program in Singapore—and other gifts of enormous size.

Cecil Day died in 1978, but his widow Deen and his children still support the work of H. I. Deen (now Mrs. Charles O. Smith, Jr.) provides the finest offices I have ever been in. I told her, "Deen, I would thank the Lord for answered prayer, but He would know that I was lying, because I never would have thought to ask the Lord for anything this nice."

A few years after my initial encounter with Cecil Day, I was reinforced in my long-held belief that whether it be a Noah, a Nehemiah, a Gideon with his 300, the four Jewish boys we read about in the Book of Daniel, or the twentieth-century Cecil Days, God does His major work through individuals and extremely small groups. I learned that by putting into practice this philosophy, the ministry of H. I. would progress much faster than if I were to wait to organize mass audiences to undergird the work.

The Gilbert-Smiths

Sometimes it seems donors come out of the woodwork. In 1986 in England, our United Kingdom executive director, Michael Penny, introduced me to Mr. and Mrs. Denham Gilbert-Smith who intended to invite some of their friends to their commodious home to hear the story of H. I. So many people responded to the invitation that the meeting had to be held at the Maidenhead Town Hall.

Denham, a forty-year-old principal with Lloyds of London, is leaving Lloyds—with their blessings, though regrets—to take full-time active leadership of the Christian Fellowship that he and some colleagues organized a few years ago.

Following the presentation about the concept and goals of H. I., the Fellowship presented me with a check for

6,000 pounds (that's over $9,100), and a check for 250 pounds to cover expenses. In addition, Denham and his wife have committed to make a personal gift of 6,000 pounds.

William Chatlos

I met William F. Chatlos when he was in his late eighties. He was a man of silence, and during our conversation I did not feel I was making headway in convincing him about the importance of the H. I. program. But his gracious daughter, Alice, responded to my conversation. He made no response.

At the end of our meeting, I led in prayer. Just as I was ready to leave, he summoned me to his office.

"Here's fifty to help you," he said handing me a check.

"Thank you," I responded. I slipped the check into my pocket. I thought it was for $50.00.

Fully persuaded that I had not made a favorable impression, I waited until I was outside his building and into my car before I looked at the check. It was for $50,000! This was the largest first-time gift the Institute has ever received.

The Lord called William Chatlos home, but his daughter and his five grandchildren have continued to support the H. I. program.

Paul Meyer

Paul Meyer, the entrepreneurial giant of Waco, Texas, has sent word to me that he is committing himself to underwrite the entire two-hundredth training session for H. I.

Not only has Paul helped enormously in providing materials, the time and expertise of Chuck Williams and, more recently, Rex Houze and Jim Schmaus, but he has also recruited friends who have given thousands of dollars.

Paul Meyer has worked with his two biographers over the past year. Neither he nor they will accept any royalties from his new book. But already, H. I. has received more than $10,000 in royalties from the Japanese edition of the book alone.

Guy W. Rutland, Jr.

Guy W. Rutland, Jr., the youngest president ever of the American Trucking Association, was a prominent man in Georgia politics. Many thought he would be governor. Although he and his wife Marie lived only nine doors from me, they had not really known about the work of H. I. until they came to one of our annual banquets in January 1974. The next day, back at the office, I was presented with a handwritten note from Guy: "I have already made out my charitable budget for 1974, and there's no slack to it. Somehow, I will try to get you $10,000."

He did. And that was just the beginning of a solid record of monthly support by this servant of God.

In addition, he served as treasurer of H. I. from 1975 until the Lord called him home in December 1986.

Arnold Browning

It was the final day of the Missions Conference at the United Presbyterian Church in San Mateo, California, October 1969, where I had brought the final messages. The senior minister, Dr. S. H. MacKenzie, invited me to his home for dinner. There I met with members of the Missions Committee including the chairperson, Mary Crawford, her husband Sam, and Amy and Arnold Browning.

They had understood the H. I. concept immediately, and they endorsed it. At that time there was no track record to which I could point, but they embraced the idea anyway. I found that refreshing. Normally, it took multiple exposures before the concept was accepted.

Dr. MacKenzie, now president of Grove City College in Pennsylvania, encouraged his people to get behind H. I. and support it. And they did. The church, the first ever to systematically support H. I., included us in their budget. The current pastor, Dr. Bob Pittman, and his people still give to this ministry.

Mary Crawford kept this ministry ever before the church, as did her successors. Arnold Browning quietly but heavily backed up the church's support not only through the budget but with increasingly generous personal and direct gifts. He did this until his death in 1986. His wife and son, John, continue Arnold's habit.

A few years ago, Arnold, with the backing of fellow board member, Mark Andre, recommended that the board members underwrite the total administration and fund-raising costs, so that all other monies would go 100 percent to the actual training of Third World leaders. To the credit of their vision and generosity, I can announce the Board adopted the Browning/Andre recommendation and have fulfilled it ever since.

I know of no Board in the world that gives year by year the number of dollars the H. I. Board gives. And they do it without fanfare.

So Many Others

The stories giving the background of the way different people became involved with H. I. are as diverse as the people themselves.

For example, Jack and Betty King, long-time friends of mine, brought a group of eight people to their home in Dallas to tell them about the Institute. Among those present were Bob and Ruth Glaze.

The Glazes began sending annual gifts. But in 1980 they called me.

"John," said Bob, "I think your concept is great. I want you to tell me more about what actually takes place. Ruth and I have been on the periphery. We intend to either get completely in or completely out. I don't get involved in anything I'm not completely sold on."

"But you've already given us thousands," I said.

"Oh, that's just a ham sandwich," said Bob.

"Bob, if you're serious, I'm leaving the end of March for

the Orient. Why don't you and Ruth come with the J. I.
McCormicks, Chris, and me to see for yourself what we're
doing."

They accepted the invitation and met face-to-face with
some of the Third World leaders meeting at Singapore. After
one of my presentations, Bob walked up to me and said, "You
can count on Ruth and me for a hundred."

He meant a hundred thousand dollars.

Once, when H. I. was in the early stages and strapped for
funds, Gordon Groth, former vice president of one of the
world's great steel companies, gave H. I. enough money to keep
it going. His reason was simple: "John," he told me, "I don't
think anybody who has not attended one of the sessions in
Singapore can conceive of the caliber of leadership represented
there. I've seen nothing in my lifetime to equal it."

There are others, so many others—Dr. G. Henry Wells,
Rev. and Mrs. Dick Hanna, Dr. C. A. Kircher, Mr. E. Harold
Keown, Sr., who worked with me from day one, to mention
a few.

Needed Funding

Why is so much funding needed? The truth of the matter is that it costs $9,100 for every leader who attends one
advanced leadership session in Singapore. The participant
pays a minimum of $300 of his own money (which is two-
months' salary in some nations); the rest is made available
through private donations.

The relatively high cost per participant is necessary because of the expense of travel (sometimes from 10,000 miles
away), the cost of room and board for a full month, the cost of
importing speakers, and the cost of a ten-year follow-up program in which we remain in contact with each graduate and
offer counsel and support of his or her work in reaching others
for the sake of the gospel.

The total cost of sponsorship for one leader of Haggai
Institute, therefore, provides:

1. Locating and Screening
2. Transportation
3. Faculty
4. Materials and Classroom Facilities
5. Lodging and Meals
6. Follow-up
7. Administrative Support

Return on Investment

In May 1986, John Bolten, a German-born American citizen, and Frank Olsen, American Broadcasting Company's head writer for fourteen years, accompanied me on a round-the-world mission.

In Seoul, Korea, I had just finished preaching to 50,000 people in the world's largest church, Central Full Gospel Church founded by Dr. Paul Yonggi Cho. At that time, they had seven Sunday services (now it's nine!) with 50,000 at each service. After the service, John Bolten said, "If I had not been here, I would not believe a church of this size existed. There's no service like this in the world." He then said, "It must be a thrill preaching to 50,000 people." He then added, "You must miss the pastorate."

"Yes, John, but I made peace with that years ago when God so fastened my mind and heart on the words of Morley, spoken in 1818, 'He who does the work is not so profitably employed as he who multiplies the doers.' I enjoy the platform. I reveled in the pastorate, but a divine call pulled me out of a ministry of addition into a ministry of multiplication.

"Now more than 4,000 have completed the Haggai Institute program, and these 4,000 have passed on their training to more than 660,000. If each of these 660,000 has influenced an average of only 10 people this week with the gospel"—John interrupted me—"I'm sure it's at least 100 from what I've observed while meeting with the graduates I've spoken to so far."

"Well, if it's 100, that means 66,000,000 people. My mathematics is not so great, but that would be 1,300 times more than I spoke to this morning—with this difference, probably 5 percent of the people this morning were non-Christians. H. I. graduates evangelize nonbelievers, many of whom know nothing about Christ."

John said, "I don't believe anybody can grasp the significance of H. I. unless he has seen the concept at work, firsthand."

After some intermediate stops, we spent time in Indonesia meeting with H. I. graduates. On the last morning, John and Frank Olsen interviewed Dr. S. J. Sutjiono while I filled another engagement. Sutjiono completed his H. I. training in 1970. I came in on the tail end of their interview.

John Bolten comes as close to being a twentieth-century Renaissance man as any person I know. He is well-bred, well educated, wealthy, a sportsman, a man of the arts, a musician, a writer, a world traveler, a multinational businessman. This extremely knowledgeable man is not easily impressed. Sutjiono's story had captivated both Bolten and Olsen.

Here are four of the highlights of Sutjiono's story:

1. He has trained more than 16,000 Indonesian leaders, and they, both lay people and clergy, work for the Lord on Indonesia's 3,000 inhabited islands.

2. Upon his return from the H. I. training he founded a church with a present membership in excess of 24,000.

3. He has written 30 major books for Christians, the general public, but especially for helpful follow-up for the 16,000 he has trained.

4. He lectures in seven departments at Indonesia's most prestigious university.

John Bolten made the point that if you divide the cost of a sponsorship, which today is $9,100, by 16,000 Sutjiono trained, and then divide that by the innumerable numbers that hear the gospel and make a decision, the H. I. method must be one of the most cost-effective means of communicating the gospel known to man today.

Sixteen thousand is five times bigger than the largest mission force today, when you realize that 25 percent of any foreign mission group are on furlough at any given time. And this 16,000 represent the work of only *one* H. I. graduate.

Finally, whenever we deal with the subject of donations, several concerns leap forward, especially in light of the 1987 scandals involving television ministries. On May 3 of that year, *The Atlanta Journal* and *The Atlanta Constitution* ran my editorial (written one year earlier) which said, in part:

> Why not request that the head of each parachurch organization make the same kind of disclosure that political candidates in the United States submit to the public?
>
> The disclosure should reveal all income and assets, including salaries, retirement benefits, housing, automobiles, airplanes, other craft for personal travel, club memberships, charge accounts paid by the organization, hospital and income replacement insurance, income and perks distributed to spouse and family members, income from board memberships, royalties on materials produced and distributed by the organization, costs to the organization of sabbaticals or long-term absences, and gifts of money, property, or materials.
>
> Above all, insist that the parachurch heads, spouses, and family members submit annually the last three income tax statements and the current net worth statements.
>
> The public deserves to know the complete financial details of the parachurch organizations they're asked to support. After all, these ministries enjoy a tax-exempt status . . . .
>
> Full disclosure is entirely consistent with the First Amendment of the Constitution. No one whose income derives from the public media has a right to financial secretiveness. Certainly not a representative of the Most High God.
>
> Such a solution . . . will enhance the credibility of the gospel that the ministries preach. As full disclosure unfrosts the opaque glass of secretiveness, Jesus Christ, whom they proclaim as the Light of the World, might even shine more brightly.

Thanks to those who support the Haggai Institute for Advanced Leadership Training the task of bringing the gospel to Third World people is being accomplished. Problems are being solved. A new door to closed countries is being opened. We are indebted to the prayers and gifts of this support group who help in continuing and expanding this work.

PART IV

THE VISION

John Haggai on the Great Wall, looking out over
China—"The dream continues"

A learned philosopher-theologian from California once wrote: "Happy is the man who dreams dreams and is ready to pay the price to make them come true." If there was ever a living example of this insight, it's John Haggai.

Beginning with a nagging urge to serve in the mission field, he was troubled because of the obvious ineffectiveness of many who were willing to give their lives for the cause of Christ. A strong faith coupled with sound logic provided the answer to the problem: We must train nationals to teach nationals. That was the dream.

A Rare Breed of Executives

Through prayer, hard work, and great personal sacrifice, he slowly but surely molded that dream into a reality.

Most people, I'm certain, would be satisfied with the results that John Haggai and his colleagues have realized. Were this a typical American business, the executives would concentrate on how to invest their earned wealth in such a way that the company could be guaranteed steady income, maintain the status quo, and, if fortunate, show a slight profit at the close of the fiscal year.

But neither John Haggai, the H. I. trustees, nor members of his staff are "typical" in any sense of the word. None of them would remain comfortable resting on their laurels. Instead, as you are reading these words, they're probably at work, brainstorming about what they can do to improve the effectiveness of their mission.

The dream—the vision—is far from over. Perhaps it will never be until the Second Coming of the Lord. And, at least from this reporter's viewpoint, the vision appears to be just as exciting as anything that has gone before.

JCM

United Kingdom Board of Directors

14

The Past Is Prologue

"In my travels throughout the world, I have encountered the strong and caring Christian influence of the Haggai Institute ministry of world evangelism. May God continue to bless this great and important work."

DR. NORMAN VINCENT PEALE

John Haggai and Bishop Athanasius of the Mar Thoma
Church, February, 1973. At the Maramon Convention, Kerala
State, India, 60,000 people attended morning prayer service

By now everyone—even those severe critics I had back in 1969—realizes that our dream for a more effective missionary outreach was not "pie in the sky." It's a pragmatic concept that works. In terms of world evangelism, I am thoroughly convinced that it is the only way that makes sense. That's why I and the entire staff of H. I. believe that we have established and continue to hone "the leading edge" in modern Christian leadership. Nearly a century ago, J. L. Nevivs, missionary to China, proposed this concept—self-government, self-propagation, self-support.

We rejoice that some denominations within the Church of our Lord have been willing to open their eyes and admit that the H. I. way is the better method in today's world. Consequently, some churchmen are attempting, even now, to duplicate these concepts in their denominations. So far, no one Church body has officially endorsed the H. I. idea of encouraging Third World leaders to determine their own programs, train their own faculty, and write their own materials. But within these denominations are groups moving in this direction.

We celebrate their support not for reasons of self-gratification, but for their willingness to suppress their collective egos and openly admit that what may have worked a hundred years ago does not necessarily work in today's global society.

We are thankful for these Christian leaders who are bold enough to take a stand in order to recommend the work they have seen. Chuck Colson (chairman of Prison Fellowship International), Ted Engstrom (president emeritus of World Vision), D. James Kennedy (president of Evangelism Explosion and founder/pastor of Coral Ridge Presbyterian Church in Fort Lauderdale, Florida) and Paul Harvey (popular national columnist and commentator), are but a few of those who have lent their names and words to the mission of the Haggai Institute.

Recently, noted pastor and author, Dr. Norman Vincent Peale, wrote: "In my travels throughout the world, I have encountered the strong and caring Christian influence of the Haggai Institute ministry of world evangelism. May God continue to bless this great and important work."

These words of endorsement by all these people of God are welcomed. But I still wish that the Church at large would echo the insight of these wise and outspoken leaders. It's sad to admit, however, that most denominations continue to wallow in their "better-than-thou" approach to world evangelism. As one former communist leader (now serving the Lord in one of Southeast Asia's great nations) recently observed, "Often their missionaries still live in expensive houses far away from the masses and ride to villages in four-wheel-drive Jeeps, while the villagers must walk miles to attend worship. Hence, without uttering one word, they leave a firm impression that the Christian faith they are eager to share with the nationals is, in reality, solely for the wealthy and Westerners."

A Plea

To those who have so far refused to alter their methods, I urge them to review what we have discovered and demonstrated to be the best way known to man for the successful work of evangelizing the Good News of Jesus Christ to Third World nations:

1. The most effective witness to a national is a fellow national. Western representatives cannot help but transmit the "Made in the U.S.A." concept.

2. The work of national evangelism must start with the leadership of the land. You build from the top down, not from the bottom up.

3. The role of the Westerner must change. It must be supportive rather than paternalistic. It must be invited, not imposed.

4. Third World Christians must come of age in terms of stewardship of money. I have never seen a strong church sustained by foreign funds.

5. Literature for evangelism in the Third World must be produced in the Third World by the Third World. This eliminates Greco-Roman thought forms of Western thinking.

6. The message must remain unaltered, but the methods must change. The Ark of the Covenant must not be tampered with, but the cart on which the Ark rests can and must be changed.

7. Leaders must be given training that relates to the needs and concerns of their nations. Like the apostle Paul, they must have the gift of motivating those to whom they pass on the message, and they must have the expertise to act based on their new knowledge and skills.

8. Any training must be done in a neutral Third World site. Leaders who study in America can be looked upon as "Uncle Toms"—whether Asian, African, or Latin.

9. The faculty must be predominantly from the Third World. We don't want the alumni to feel they have been tainted by a "foreign culture."

10. The selection of leaders must be the result of careful screening. They must be evangelical, able to speak and read English, agree to transfer their studies to their own people upon return to their land, and must not be engaged in any activities against their government.

11. The results must be measured. I have seen evidence

of people reading their Bibles regularly (who never did before), of attendance at churches increasing three and four times the usual number in just a few short months, and of lay people willing to lay down their lives for the sake of the gospel.

A Revealing Breakfast

One morning in 1976 Cecil Day invited me to breakfast with one of the world's most respected mission leaders—a man whom I had admired for years. As we sat in Cecil's private dining room, the mission leader took the conversational initiative. He insisted that his denomination had been training Third World leaders for a hundred years.

I knew he was mistaken. I knew the mission philosophy of his denomination. But out of respect for Cecil I said nothing. Before my cup of coffee grew cold, I thought to myself: *Well, there goes Cecil's support of H. I.*

Later that afternoon, I bumped into Cecil in an elevator. Cecil, a man of few, but pointed, words looked at me and said, "Thanks for joining me at breakfast, John." Then he paused and added, "They just don't understand, do they?"

That reminded me of how often we underestimate the insight of such devout lay people.

I challenge anyone to find fault with the H. I. approach to effective evangelism in the Third World. The effectiveness of the past is but a prologue to the future if we allow it to work. The only alternative we have is to continue the way we've been striving throughout the centuries. The late W. B. Camp of Bakersfield, California, fourteen years an officer of the United States Chamber of Commerce, said, "You can't use yesterday's methods in today's world and be in business tomorrow."

Too often, all many major denominations can point to for their accomplishments is that the ditch to which Bob Pierce referred—in which many of their dedicated missionaries continue to walk—only gets deeper and deeper.

Is this what Jesus had in mind when He gave us the "Great Commission"?

15

Dreams Become Tormenting Visions

"The Haggai Institute has set a goal—an ambitious, but clearly attainable goal—to train 10,000 leaders before the year 2000."

JOHN HAGGAI

Bishop Chandu Ray from Karachi, Pakistan—
Haggai Institute faculty anchorman and lecturer

To date, over 4,800 world leaders from 96 nations have completed study at the Haggai Institute. Had anyone told me that back in 1969 when we conducted our first session in Switzerland, I would have questioned his sanity. But, by the grace of Almighty God, that's exactly what has taken place.

A lot has been accomplished, certainly, but there remains so much yet to do. As of this moment, an estimated three fourths of the Third World's people still live in countries that either bureaucratically discourage or openly prohibit foreign missionary efforts.

Tormenting Visions

In this regard, our dreams of the past have turned into tormenting visions for the future. What would result, for instance, were we at H. I. to lay back, pat ourselves on the back, and cease to grow? The answer is obvious: We would return to the former ways of doing things—sending the white, Anglo-Saxon Westerner into Third World nations in an anemic attempt to introduce nationals to the gospel of Jesus Christ. And

the results would be the same: In spite of the missionaries'
pleas that Christ died for all nations, Christianity would be
looked upon as "the White Man's faith."

The Haggai Institute has set a goal—an ambitious but
clearly attainable goal—to train 10,000 leaders before the year
2000. Because every alumnus also shares his training with
at least 100 others on the average (some have trained thousands), the mission force of trained evangelists will surpass
one million.

I rejoice to say that everyone on the H. I. staff is committed to evangelism. Our donors, faculty, secretaries, alumni,
executive staff, and board are dedicated to the proposition that
every man, woman, and child needs to hear the Good News of
the Lord, Jesus Christ.

Sometime ago, on a television talk show, my interviewer
queried, "Do I understand you to mean that Jesus Christ is just
about the only answer to almost every problem confronting
man today?"

"No," I replied. "If I left that impression, I apologize, and
want to correct it right now."

The interviewer responded, "I thought I must have misunderstood you. Surely you don't believe that Jesus Christ is just
about the only answer to almost every problem confronting
man."

"That's right," I said. "I believe Jesus Christ is the *only*
answer to *every* problem confronting man today."

The Bible makes this clear. History underscores it. Personal experience corroborates it. It seems that the only thing
we learn from history is that we don't learn anything from
history.

Who did more for education than Russell Conwell? His
concern originated with his commitment to Jesus Christ. His
work in education and the establishment of Temple University
have impacted upon every continent for good.

Who did more for the working man than England's Lord
Shaftesbury? His concern originated with his commitment
to Christ.

Who did more for social reform than John Wesley? His effectiveness originated with his Aldersgate experience when he committed his life to the Lord Jesus at the age of 38, after he had taught at Oxford and served as a missionary to the colony of Georgia.

Who did more for youth, through his personal ministry and through the Y.M.C.A., than Dwight L. Moody? His great work originated with his commitment to Christ.

Who did more for the poor than General William Booth and his Salvation Army? His concern originated with his commitment to Christ.

In his day, who did more for the black man than William Wilberforce, the man who single-handedly rammed through the British Parliament a bill in 1805 bringing an end to slave-trading? His concern began with his commitment to Christ in a John Wesley revival meeting.

Who did more to change the social, moral, and political complexion of Southeast Asia than Dr. John Sung? His unparalleled influence for good began with his commitment to Christ.

Who has so influenced the great nation of Korea with its unprecedented spiritual revival, its proliferation of orphanages, universities, hospitals, and beneficent penetration in all areas of society than Dr. Han Kyung Chik? Dr. Paul Yonggi Cho, pastor of the world's largest church (over 600,000 members) lauds Dr. Han as God's inspiration to all Koreans. His great work began with his commitment to Jesus Christ.

Haggai Institute's program of evangelism not only reveals this same faith to Third World people, but also gives every listener a chance to respond to it by accepting Jesus Christ as personal Savior.

Philosophical Approaches

The Grecian says, "Man, know thyself." The Roman says, "Man, rule thyself." The Chinese says, "Man, improve thyself." The Buddhist says, "Man, annihilate thyself." The Brahman says, "Man, submerge thyself in the universal sum of it all." The twentieth-century internationalist says, "Man, learn the art and practice the principles of peaceful coexistence." But Christ says, "Without me, you can do nothing."

There's no question that our entire staff shares this faith. There's no doubt that our faculty members constantly go above and beyond the call of duty to offer the best training to Third World nationals. But if we are to reach our goal of 10,000 by the year 2000, we have to expand, pure and simple.

The facilities in Singapore can train only a few hundred leaders a year. We cannot expand the school in Singapore because of building restrictions. Therefore, our only alternative is to find another location. But where?

We could build a center somewhere in the continental United States. In fact, we've been offered free land were we to do this. But any location within these boundaries would be tainted with the Western look. At the same time, a location closer for South American and Pacific Rim leaders would offer a tremendous advantage in terms of the time and cost of travel.

After months of intense investigation, we found an ideal location near Honolulu, Hawaii, America's Asian state.

Although it's part of the United States, Hawaii is not identified with Westernized America. In addition, its locale creates far less travel problems for the leaders of South America.

Land has already been purchased, and the new, modern buildings will soon be ready for occupancy.

With the new center in Hawaii, the program of the Haggai Institute for Advanced Leadership Training can graduate twice the alumni at a reduced overhead for each graduate. That means more souls reached with the Good News of the gospel.

Beyond Hawaii are other dreams.

But, that's another story.